COMING ALIVE
from Nine to Five

The Career Search Handbook

Betty Neville Michelozzi
CAREER COUNSELOR
WEST VALLEY COLLEGE

 MAYFIELD PUBLISHING COMPANY

Library of Congress Catalog Card Number: 79-89921
International Standard Book Number: 0-87484-482-7

Manufactured in the United States of America
Mayfield Publishing Company
285 Hamilton Avenue, Palo Alto, California 94301

This book was set in VIP Souvenir Light and Helvetica Light by
Hansen Associates and was printed and bound by the George
Banta Company. Sponsoring editor was Robert W. Erhart,
Carole Norton supervised editing and Carol King was manuscript editor. The book was designed by Nancy Sears and cover
and chapter opening art are by Tom Durfee. Michelle Hogan
supervised production.

Contents

Preface

Career search can be a very special and precious time to orient and organize our lives. It can be a time when we look deeply at ourselves and what we have been doing. It can lead us to question how we intend to spend our lives for a time, or our time for the rest of our lives: to keep or not to keep certain goals, to change or not to change certain behaviors, to aspire or not to aspire to certain positions—all with a view toward greater life enrichment.

Career search can be more than simply figuring out what job might suit us best. That is the short-range view. The perspective expands when we ask ourselves what we want the job to do for us. Very quickly we can find ourselves face to face with some of our deepest values. Do we want money, power, status? Peace, harmony, love? Are some values incompatible with others? Can we have it all?

Can we work sixty hours a week while moving up the corporate ladder, nurture loving relationships with family and friends, grow our own vegetables, recycle tin cans on Saturdays, jog daily, be a Scout leader, meditate, and do yoga? How fully can all of our interests and values be actualized in the real world? What is the purpose of work? What is the purpose of life?

Career search, then, can be a profound journey of personal growth—not just a superficial choosing and securing of a job. What is needed is a system that is clear and demystified: First, a system that helps people to articulate who they are and what they do well. Second, a system that describes the work world as simply as possible. Third, a system that assists searchers to see the relationship between their personal characteristics and that world of work. And finally, a system that "empowers" them to secure the job they have decided upon by increasing their awareness of the basic elements of good job hunting.

Coming Alive from Nine to Five is an attempt to develop, demystify, and integrate between two covers these various facets of career search and choice. It is meant to be a comprehensive handbook: a handy reference book drawing together

ix

into one practical, easily useable and re-useable source the essentials of the process. It is flexible enough to be used in whole or in part, in individual counseling sessions, in workshops, or in semester-long courses.

The handbook is intended for anyone who is making a life change. While it focuses specifically on careers, this topic can be translated into meaningful life activity. The book contains valuable material for all phases of career choice even into retirement. Close to 2,000 copies of the manuscript have been tested for the last two years by practitioners in various settings. It has been used successfully by a broad population of all ages and backgrounds: from high school students to persons approaching retirement; from welfare mothers to affluent housewives; from CETA trainees to career-changing professionals.

Serious career search calls for commitment and motivation. This is particularly true for searchers who attempt to use this handbook on their own. Yet serious though it is, paradoxically the process is most fruitful if approached in a relaxed, lighthearted manner. In any case, it is important for users to become thoroughly involved in it. Those who do so will experience greater clarity about themselves and new confidence in themselves. Their goals will become easier to recognize and to reach, and they will move farther along the path of self-actualization. Their career search will become a journey of personal growth. And they will come alive from nine to five!

Acknowledgments

☞ **Private: Please do not read this**

Acknowledgments are a very personal thing. They point up the fact that it is impossible to accomplish anything of importance all alone. Thanks to:

Peter, my husband, for his honest feedback and endless reading and listening, his help with developing some of the surveys and the job market material. This work has motivated him to do dishes often, vacuum, make great salads, and many other neat things.

All the caring, careful *typists* from Nan Halterman, the typing classes of Barbara Lea and Donnette Dake, Shirley Rosenberg, Elaine Rivas, Teresa Salazar, and proofreader Virginia Smith, to Phyllis Newton, Ruby Garcia, and Kay Koyano; and publications facilitators: Ed Sherry, Al Hull, Mickey Wesmacott, Gayle Amato, Mary Rocher, Beth Weslow, and Jennifer Pelham.

Supportive *colleagues* who read, reviewed, and gave helpful feedback: Bill Allman, Veronese Anderson, Chloe Atkins, Don Cordero, Ken Gogstad, Jo Hernandez, Michael Herauf, Joyce Hinkle, Sharon Johnson, Gladys Penner, Pat Space, Peter Thelin, Pat Weber, Jan Winton, all from West Valley; Ronald Arroyo, Ken Blaker, Tat Blesch, Ann Bowers, Liza Caton-Egnew, Jim Gordon, Clare Holt, Bette Kent, John Maginley, Glen McRae, Ruth Morales, Phyllis Sutphen, Garland White, Judith White, Susanna Yamat. Academic reviewers who contributed valuable suggestions and comments: William Mitchell of California State University, Sacramento, Bruce Shertzer of Purdue University, and Benjamin J. Shumaker of Macomb County Community College.

West Valley College *students* who taught me to teach Careers and Lifestyles and shared the beauty of their lives and their journeys.

The people at Mayfield who were so supportive and helpful: Bob Erhart, Pamela Trainer, Carole Norton, Carol King, and Nancy Sears.

My family and friends who gave me "living love." You have all enriched me.

Betty

xi

Introduction

A career is an important and vital means of self-expression. Besides a means of earning a living, a career can be a way to satisfy some of our deepest needs. Getting in touch with oneself—one's needs, wants, feelings, and values—is an important first step toward personal growth in the search for one's career.

You are here, reading this book, because you are a searcher. Somehow you've discovered that work/life can be meaningful/rewarding/satisfying/fulfilling. You want to make wise choices. You need to know yourself and what you enjoy before you choose. In this book you will look at, evaluate, and ponder various aspects of your life: your needs and how they relate to your wants, your feelings and reasoned judgment, your values, your interests and skills. Ultimately, all of these determine our actions and the very fabric of our lives. Relating this information to the world of work can result in better decisions for the whole of your life.

Career choice sometimes seems like a trivial thing. We ask six-year-olds what they want to be when they grow up. Are they going to sell shoes at Kinney's or invade the corporate complex of IBM? Will plumbing be their outlet or travel tours their bag?

But at least occasionally, the image of life's wholeness flashes before us and we see a large, work-filled part of it stretching into the future. We catch a glimpse of the time and energy that we will invest in work. We see that work will affect our lives in many ways. Unless we keep a tight lid on it, the ultimate question will eventually present itself: "What's it all about, Alfie?" If we deal in depth with career choice, we are bound to slip into a philosophic consideration of life's meaning. To do otherwise is to trivialize a profound experience.

At first glance this book looks like a conventional careers manual. Read it, fill in the blanks, and (even if you're already over forty) you'll know what you want to be when you grow up.

You *will* find blanks to fill in as part of the step-by-step process of getting to know yourself and the job world. You will explore your needs, wants, and values. You will discover your personality orientation. You will examine your past and select those activities you've enjoyed, as well as skills you've developed over the years. A job group chart will help you to put *you* and *work* together in a meaningful way. And a final inventory will collect all this "you data" and help you to see it as a unified whole.

But this book also touches on some of the heavier issues of life. How can you fulfill your potential? Be happy? Be content? It deals with such things lightly—sometimes whimsically—because life is joyful. But after a good chuckle we get serious and *think* again because our lives are also important and sometimes sad.

The career search is really a time to *stop out* to see who you are and where you're *growing*. This text was written for those who are in transition and would like the opportunity to learn a thought-full career decision process: graduating seniors, women no longer needed at home, the newly divorced or widowed, job changers, the disabled, the unemployed, grandmothers and grandfathers kicking up their heels, corporate tycoons stopping to smell the flowers, people in midlife crises, veterans, ex-clerics, people becoming parents and providers, persons retiring, and all others who are willing to let go of no longer appropriate behaviors and risk new ones.

A book about career choice is inevitably a book about life and all its stages from 19 to 99.

FENWICK

Reprinted with permission Washington Star Syndicate, Inc.

COMING ALIVE from Nine to Five
The Career Search Handbook

One — Needs, wants, and values:

T. DURFEE

Spotlighting YOU

The best place to start a growth process is at its roots. Ask yourself what you really *need*. A genuine need is something you must have to survive, something you cannot live without. And after your basic needs are identified, begin to look at your *wants*. Wants enrich life beyond the level of needs. What we want reflects our *values* and gives meaning to our lives. Looking at needs, wants, and values, at the roots of a career search, can open a new phase of personal growth.

Abraham Maslow, who arranged human needs into a famous hierarchy, stated that basic, lower needs *must* be at least minimally fulfilled before one can move toward self-actualization.

Physiological needs are the most basic. Without air, for example, we wouldn't survive many minutes. Gandhi said, "Even God cannot talk to a hungry man except in terms of bread."

Next, we must feel reasonably safe in order to get on with the business of living. It would be hard to concentrate on reading a great book in a burning building. But our physical safety can be threatened in many remote ways too. We can let ourselves worry about future possibilities like illness from air pollution and chemical additives, our care in old age, meeting new and unfamiliar situations, and job security. Such continued worry can shrivel our energy.

Yet we've heard stories about infants orphaned by war whose physical and safety needs were met, but nevertheless they mysteriously died. We've heard of old people "dying of loneliness" or of a person in a concentration camp dying after hearing of the death of a loved one. Human beings seem to need love; some kind of faith and assurance that they are lovable, that someone cares; someone with whom they can exchange affection; someone to give them courage. People's self-esteem can be badly damaged by real or imagined love deprivation. Their life energy seems to be diminished.

3

However, Maslow said, "Even if all these needs are satisfied, we may still often (if not always) expect that a new discontent and restlessness will soon develop, unless the individual is doing what he's fitted for. A musician must make music, an artist must paint, a poet must write, if he is to be ultimately at peace with himself. What a man can be, he must be. This need we call self actualization."[1]

A self-actualized person, then, has solved most of life's problems. The human person is born to grow, to be open in spirit, to become self-actualized. Like a tree, we can't grow backwards. No matter where we are or what our past has been, we can get to a better place.

✳ ✳ ✳ ✳ ✳ ✳ ✳ ✳ ✳ ✳ ✳ ✳ ✳

T H E   U N E X A M I N E D
life is not worth living.
—SOCRATES

✳ ✳ ✳ ✳ ✳ ✳ ✳ ✳ ✳ ✳ ✳ ✳ ✳

Needs relate to wants

Every human being is located somewhere on the road that leads to self-actualization. We spend a great deal of time trying to see our way. Yet at times we find ourselves "half-way down the block" before we realize we've turned the corner. Careful self-assessment will help you become more conscious of your path, more in tune with your own inner rhythms. You will become more aware of your uniqueness.

All human beings have essentially the same needs, but obviously we vary in even the most basic of these. A 200-pound man will need more oxygen than a six-pound baby. In addition, our basic needs are expressed as a complex variety of wants, which in turn express our individuality. Water will quench thirst, but some people want martinis.

According to the O'Neils in *Shifting Gears*,[2] it is important to distinguish between what we want and what we need. Once we know the difference, we won't feel that we have to have everything we want. Our wants won't control us. We can prefer something and work to obtain it without demanding it addictively.

The complexity of human wants defies description. Furthermore, our wants can become the saboteurs of our needs. A prime example is the use of possessions to fulfill love needs. Hoping that status symbols will make us valued, we want sports cars, big houses, and important jobs. By flaunting material possessions, however, we may alienate the very people we are trying to impress. What we really want is their love.

Needs and wants relate to feelings

How did our own individual sets of wants come to be? Basically, they came from two divergent areas: what feels good to us and the reasoned and not-so-reasoned judgment of others.

Running free feels good to a child, but the reasoned judgment of an adult says that a busy street is not a good place to exercise this freedom. The child learns to curb good feelings in the face of good judgment. Exploring and taking risks feels good to a child. Reasoned judgment would advise checking ahead. But if not-so-reasoned judgment and excess caution inspire anxiety about every venture, the child will lose the joy of trying new things.

As adults, then, we need to look at the things we want and value—things that are important to us. On the one hand, we need to see if we are acting on feelings and sabotaging our real needs by not using reasoned judgment. On the other hand, the opposite may be true: by absorbing the not-too-reasoned judgments of others, we may have lost touch with some things that would give us joy. We are afraid of our feelings, or we have exchanged true feelings for unreal fear or frustration.

When we try to ignore feelings and shift attention away from them, they may come out in inappropriate ways. We explode over a minor irritation because we've been "saving up" our anger. We can experience bodily tension by denying feelings —sometimes to such an extent that we become ill. It is difficult to exercise good judgment and make life decisions when feelings are troublesome. Learning to deal in a straightforward way with feelings is an important growth step.

Carl Rogers, who first used the term "unconditional positive regard," believes that a person grows best and most positively when he or she can explore feelings freely in a caring, nonjudgmental atmosphere. If we assume that feelings are a physiological phenomenon, we cannot judge others' feelings, but must accept them as useful indicators. Anger, love, and fear are physical reactions to our environment. By focusing directly on these feelings, experiencing them, and sharing and exploring them with others, we can learn to channel our emotional energy and use it in a more effective way.

All personal growth activities are aimed at better understanding oneself in relationship to others and the environment. When I begin to understand myself, I can learn to take responsibility for what I feel. Instead of blaming others for what I feel, I may realize that my troublesome reactions are largely based on past experiences instead of present realities. I may catch myself misinterpreting another's words or actions and thinking the worst, without checking the facts.

Self-deception results when one feeling masks another. Suppose I feel angry at a meeting when someone speaks well, expressing an idea I couldn't put into words. My anger may mask hurt pride. My hurt pride may mask feelings of inferiority and insecurity, which in turn mask a profound feeling of being unesteemed by others. If I learned to recognize the truth, I might say, "I feel profoundly unesteemed when others articulate ideas well." This statement puts me in touch with an absurdity and helps me to become aware of my esteem needs. I may then find ways to meet my needs. And incidentally, I may become aware that I seldom, if ever, compliment or give esteem to others.

If I care about my relationships with others, I will share my feelings with them when appropriate in an honest and caring way, taking responsibility for the feelings, and experiencing them without denial or delay so that I can deal with them clearly. I will be neither timid nor aggressive but assertive. Both the timid and the aggressive person create dissonance wherever they go: one by "nitpicking around the bush," the other by bulldozing the bush out of existence. And who wants to spend a lifetime "picking nits or dozing bulls?" (Some of us alternate between the two

THE TIMID PERSON	THE ASSERTIVE PERSON	THE AGGRESSIVE PERSON
is	*is*	*is*
indirect, inhibited self-conscious, unsure	direct, clear, open, centered, accepting	direct, overbearing, domineering, controlling, insensitive
and feels	*and feels*	*and feels*
tearful, shaky, angry, hurt	strong, buoyant, self-respecting, confident	angry, explosive; superior, demanding, pseudo-confident
and experiences	*and experiences*	*and experiences*
uncertainty, domination, disregard, disrespect, annoyance from others.	acceptance, clarity, respect, cooperation from others.	lack of cooperation, isolation, confusion, anger, hurt, guilt from others.

extremes: first being polite and suppressing our feelings, and then exploding.) The assertive person, on the other hand, is a growing, balanced person who is centered within self, feels comfortable with life, has little need to fear or control people, is more able to love and value self and others. Such a person more than likely will be loved and valued.

As we become more clear about what we feel and balance those feelings with good judgment, we are becoming aware of what we cherish most in life. Decision-making and action are easier when we know what we value and when we recognize the order of our priorities. We are then able to seek, search, and risk. In the words of Ken Keyes, Jr., we thus create our own world, and "a loving person lives in a loving world."[3]

Needs, wants, feelings relate to values

What I *need* is an absolute survival minimum.

What I *want* goes beyond survival to a place of enriched choices.

What I *feel* gets me in touch with needs and wants and helps me to consider what I really *value*.

Becoming aware of what we really value and cherish is a lifetime process. To find out whether an action of yours truly reflects a value, ask yourself if

- you had a choice
- you weighed your choices carefully
- you chose freely
- you are happy with your choice
- it has become a part of your life pattern.

Values are what we *do*, not what we *say*. Our struggles, disappointments, worries, hopes, and dreams are all indicators of value areas. And also, a true set of values is indicated when we feel confident, enthusiastic, and clear about ourselves and others.

On the other hand, murky values can result in many conflicts. We see these conflicts in people who are apparently turned off, confused, changeable, complaining, alienated, or "lazy." The person who over-conforms or over-rebels probably has problems clarifying values.

The values each person cherishes are an individual expression of self. For King Midas, gold was everything. Most people are astounded when someone leaves a million dollars to a pet cat.

All aspects of life are value-laden. Here, for example, are some areas important in our value systems: family, love and friendship, religion and virtue, work and leisure.[4]

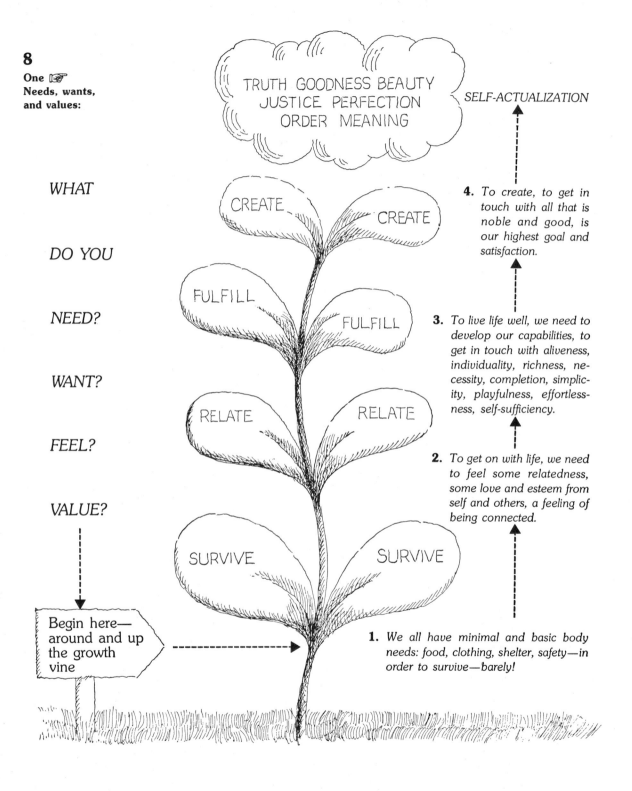

WHAT

DO YOU

NEED?

WANT?

FEEL?

VALUE?

Begin here—
around and up
the growth
vine

TRUTH GOODNESS BEAUTY
JUSTICE PERFECTION
ORDER MEANING

SELF-ACTUALIZATION

CREATE   CREATE

FULFILL   FULFILL

RELATE   RELATE

SURVIVE   SURVIVE

4. *To create, to get in touch with all that is noble and good, is our highest goal and satisfaction.*

3. *To live life well, we need to develop our capabilities, to get in touch with aliveness, individuality, richness, necessity, completion, simplicity, playfulness, effortlessness, self-sufficiency.*

2. *To get on with life, we need to feel some relatedness, some love and esteem from self and others, a feeling of being connected.*

1. *We all have minimal and basic body needs: food, clothing, shelter, safety—in order to survive—barely!*

Personal growth

Getting re-acquainted with ourselves—our feelings, needs, wants, and our most cherished values—is a continuous process. But at certain stages of life the quest for self becomes imperative. We find that we have grown out of familiar roles: nurturer, business dynamo, provider, supermom. Certain images of ourselves no longer fit. Life also has a way of forcing us to make changes. When children start school, and especially when they leave home, a person can no longer be a parent in the same old sense. When a young person graduates from college, takes a job, marries and has children, he/she can no longer be a full-time, carefree young adult. When a person achieves success in a job and reaches the top or realizes he/she is not going to reach the top, what then?

Growing as a person means changing, adjusting to both inner and outer reality. It means expansion into new and exciting areas of life. Never before in the history of humankind have people had such opportunity for growth at later stages of life, simply because people have never lived this long. Child rearing and supporting was just about all there was. Very old people were rare.

HERMAN *by Unger*

Maturity is a feeling that comes over you when you look back on your life and realize you were wrong on just about everything.

We are slowly beginning to perceive a new dimension to our lives. We see people going back to school at 70 and 80, getting degrees, starting businesses, publishing their first books, painting, initiating nationwide political action groups, teaching swimming! We are confused: what ever happened to that obsolete object, the rocking chair? People are discovering that their powers are about as strong as their attitudes: physical (including sexual) ability, the ability to learn, to grow and develop new ideas. Limits seem to be vanishing like desert mirages. My mother went to work at a publishing company at age 70 with not much training or work experience. Her success at correcting material and supervising other workers was a source of amazement and delight to her.

The alternative to growth is: a diminished life that closes out *self* by put-downs, lack of confidence, many "shoulds"; closes out *others* by bitter, angry thoughts, blaming/projecting, many "shoulds"; closes out *life* by tension, anxiety, and finding fault on all sides.

Personal growth means: not getting stuck at the crossroads, but moving on; not clinging to an obsolete role, but trying on new ones until one fits; not denying, but accepting reality.

Times of transition are fearful periods when life seems so empty that we'd give anything not to face reality. But when we do face it, we are amazed at how much more there is of all good and joyful things, especially love for ourselves and others. We gradually begin to see life differently. Self-awareness leads to self-acceptance, which leads to self-confidence. We are on the way to self-actualization.

A self-actualized person* might be described as follows:

- An authentic, open person
- Not defensive or "phony"
- Has no need for roles or masks
- Simple, natural, with little use for "trappings"
- Autonomous, centered, not pulled along with every fad
- Able to make decisions, take responsibility
- Spontaneous, passionate, creative, enjoyer of life, yet moral, ethical, concerned
- Takes life seriously with a generous touch of whimsy
- Can see through the "put ons" of others with a benign view and maybe even a chuckle
- Emotionally balanced—enjoying peak experiences, delighting in people, art, and nature, yet able to "get the job done"
- Not burdened with anxiety, guilt, or shame
- Takes time for self-renewal and relaxation
- Can be alone or in a group with equal ease
- Values privacy, yet feels one with humankind

*Data and summary from Hierarchy of Needs in "A Theory of Human Motivation" in *Motivation and Personality*, 2nd Edition by Abraham H. Maslow, Copyright © 1970 by Abraham H. Maslow. By permission of Harper & Row, Publishers, Inc.

- Tends to form deep personal relationships based on love and caring with other self-actualizing people
- Has a basic set of beliefs, a philosophy of life[5]

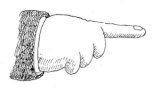

EXERCISES: SPOTLIGHTING YOU

The following exercises are designed to help you with your inward search. *Use only the ones that seem useful to you. You may not need to do them all.* They will help you explore your feelings, needs, wants, and values. A self-portrait section will assist you to look at your "free-spirit years," school experiences, and various periods in your life. Various ideas for an autobiography can be used to help with life planning. From this you can see how you've been having fun all your life and what has been most satisfying.

At the very end of this manual you will find a section set aside for summaries of the exercises. You may put the results of your surveys there as you go along. Or you may wait until you reach the end of the book and then go back and collect them all. It's up to you.

1. Tapping into feelings

The first three exercises give you a chance to tap into your feelings about *you* and other people and to check areas that could be problems to you. Growth can result from looking at these things and choosing which ones you'd like to change. Much of career choice involves *admitting*, at least to yourself, how you *really* feel.

A. Check the words that describe you most of the time:

_____ Confused	_____ Satisfied	_____ Depressed
_____ Happy	_____ Stimulated	_____ Serious
_____ Confident	_____ Calm	_____ Apathetic
_____ Worried	_____ Weary	_____ Cynical
_____ Loving	_____ Disgusted	_____ Agitated
_____ Skeptical	_____ Discouraged	_____ Withdrawn
_____ Encouraged	_____ Fearful	_____ Angry
_____ Involved	_____ Quiet	_____ Violent
_____ Frustrated	_____ Bored	_____ Not sure

B. Check those groups with whom you feel most comfortable:

_____ Students

_____ People your own age

_____ Younger people

_____ Older people

_____ Your family

_____ Your friends

_____ The middle class

_____ Liberals

_____ People of your religion

_____ People of your neighborhood

_____ People of your nationality

_____ People of your race

_____ Working class

_____ Conservatives

_____ Intellectuals

_____ People concerned about personal growth

_____ People of backgrounds different from yours

_____ High status people

_____ Artistic people

_____ Others

C. Double check any problem areas from A and B you would like to change.

D. Rate the items below by checking the appropriate column:

A   no problem—happy there

B   slight problem

Y   moderate problem

Z   a considerable problem

Year +   a great problem for more than a year

Chronic   a problem throughout your life

	A	B	Y	Z	Year +	Chronic
1. Parents/brothers/sisters						
2. Spouse/children						
3. Family closeness						
4. Friends/relationships/love						
5. Privacy/freedom						
6. Dwelling						
7. Work						
8. Finances						
9. Personal achievement/success						
10. Confidence						
11. Health						
12. Diet/drugs/drinking/smoking						
13. Exercise						
14. Your appearance						
15. Physical well-being						
16. Hectic lifestyle						
17. Recreation/hobbies						
18. Spiritual/religious well-being						
19. Emotional/mental well-being						
20. Status						
21. Intellectual ability						
22. Artistic ability						
23. Education						
24. Social concern						
25. Political concern						

Circle the numbers of items you would like to change. Perhaps see a counselor to discuss your feelings. It's easier to make a good career decision if anxieties are not getting in the way.

14

2. Needs and wants

A. Survival needs plus

What lifestyle is important to you?

Dream—let your imagination soar—describe your ideal.

Your home _____

Your clothing _____

Your food _____

Your family _____

Your friends _____

Your associates _____

Your transportation _____

Your pets/plants _____

Your gadgets and playthings _____

Your activities _____

Other _____

B. People needs

What do you expect from each group around you? What would you like to change?

_____

_____

_____

_____

C. Fulfillment needs

Dream again! If you could instantly have your way, already trained and skilled, what would you do:

a. to amaze your friends and family?

_____

_____

_____

b. to delight yourself?

_____

_____

_____

c. to improve the world?

_____

_____

_____

D. _Today_, what immediate steps, little or big, can you take to improve your life?

_____

_____

_____

_____

_____

3. Exploring your values

The next four exercises are designed to help you become aware of what you value in life.* Use only the ones that seem useful to *you*.

A. Enjoyment values

List 20 things you love to do.

Mark each according to the following code:

A   alone

P   with people

A–P   both alone and with others

$ if it costs more than $5 each time

____	1. _____	____	11. _____
____	2. _____	____	12. _____
____	3. _____	____	13. _____
____	4. _____	____	14. _____
____	5. _____	____	15. _____
____	6. _____	____	16. _____
____	7. _____	____	17. _____
____	8. _____	____	18. _____
____	9. _____	____	19. _____
____	10. _____	____	20. _____

Top five:

1. ____   2. ____   3. ____   4. ____   5. ____

B. Life values

Below is a list of 18 values arranged in alphabetical order. Your task is to arrange them in order of their importance to *you* as guiding principles in *your* life.

Study the list carefully. Then place a 1 next to the value that is most important for *you*; place a 2 next to the second most important, and so on. The value that is least important, relative to the others, should be ranked 18.

Work slowly and think carefully. If you change your mind, feel free to change your answers. The end result should show how you really feel.

_____ *A comfortable life* (a prosperous life)

_____ *Equality* (brotherhood, equal opportunity for all)

_____ *An exciting life* (a stimulating, active life)

_____ *Family security* (taking care of loved ones)

_____ *Freedom* (independence, free choice)

_____ *Happiness* (contentedness)

_____ *Inner harmony* (freedom from inner conflict)

_____ *Mature love* (sexual and spiritual intimacy)

_____ *National security* (protection from attack)

_____ *Pleasure* (an enjoyable, leisurely life)

_____ *Salvation* (deliverance from sin, eternal life)

_____ *Self-respect* (self-esteem)

_____ *A sense of accomplishment* (making a lasting contribution)

_____ *Social recognition* (respect, admiration)

_____ *True friendship* (close companionship)

_____ *Wisdom* (a mature understanding of life)

_____ *A world at peace* (freedom from war and conflict)

_____ *A world of beauty* (beauty of nature and the arts)

C. Personal trait values

Rank order the following values from 1 to 17.

_____ *Ambitious* (hard-working, aspiring)

_____ *Broadminded* (open-minded)

_____ *Capable* (competent, effective)

_____ *Cheerful* (lighthearted, joyful)

_____ *Clean* (neat, tidy)

_____ *Courageous* (standing up for your beliefs)

_____ *Forgiving* (willing to pardon others)

_____ *Helpful* (working for the welfare of others)

_____ *Honest* (sincere, truthful)

_____ *Imaginative* (daring, creative)

_____ *Independent* (self-reliant, self-sufficient)

_____ *Intellectual* (intelligent, reflective)

_____ *Logical* (consistent, rational)

_____ *Loving* (affectionate, tender)

_____ *Obedient* (dutiful, respectful)

_____ *Polite* (courteous, well-mannered)

_____ *Self-controlled* (restrained, self-disciplined)

D. Career values

The following is a list of 18 values related to work. Rank them 1 to 18 in order of importance to you.

_____ *Being secure*

_____ *Having fun*

_____ *Having status*

_____ *Designing systems*

_____ *Helping people*

_____ *Being physically active*

_____ *Making things*

_____ *Creating ideas*

_____ *Being independent*

_____ *Taking risks*

_____ *Creating beauty*

_____ *Exploring ideas*

_____ *Following directions*

_____ *Taking responsibility*

_____ *Experiencing variety*

_____ *Making money*

_____ *Improving society*

_____ *Organizing things*

Your career values are an expression of personal values. If your values are clear, it will be easier to choose careers that are in harmony with Y–O–U.

4. Draw a self-portrait

Many people find it helpful, when making a life change, to review their past experiences. An important clue to your skills and interests is to become aware of what you've been doing all your life. Pay attention to what gave you pleasure and satisfaction. Your disappointments are important too, since they wouldn't be disappointing if they meant nothing to you. Some people find great motivation striving for success in a so-called area of failure. The following exercises are designed to help you recall some important happenings in your life.

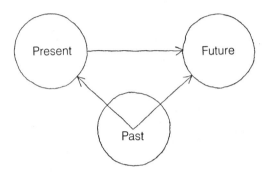

A. Your free-spirit years

One important time was your pre-teen years when you were a "free spirit." At about age five or six you began to be independent enough to cross the street alone and make some choices. During that time you may have chosen friends and activities without too much parental guidance. You weren't too worried about what people thought. What did you enjoy most during those years?

Make a list of activities you were involved with when you were 5 to 10 years old. Remember various seasons, indoors, outdoors; remember friends you played with. Check the things you enjoyed most.

_____   _____

_____   _____

_____   _____

_____   _____

_____   _____

_____   _____

B. School subjects

To get in touch further with your past, check the columns that describe your feelings about school subjects:

	Like	Dislike	Did well	Did not do well	Avoided
Reading					
Writing					
Speech/Drama					
Math					
Science					
Social studies					
Art/Crafts					
Music					
Industrial/Technical					
Business					
Health					
Agriculture					
Physical education					
Any others?					

Circle the subjects you'd like to study further.

Now look at your "worst" subjects. Are there any that you'd like to try again? Few people have the time and energy to become good at everything. But often our work is poor only because we don't want to make the effort to improve. Getting rid of this "excess baggage" can be a liberating experience.

C. Autobiographical summary

List the important events and successes in each period of your life. List disappointments with reference to family, school, friends, work, and whatever else you wish.

	Important events	Successes	Disappointments
Young childhood			
Elementary school			
High school			
Young adulthood/college			

	Important events	Successes	Disappointments
Marriage/career decisions			
Family involvement			
The middle years ("Is there life after 40?")			
The silver and golden years			

D. An autobiography

Many people find that doing an autobiography is a valuable way to re-discover themselves. Here are several suggestions.

1. You could simply *write* one telling the story of your life.

2. Or you could use the three circles and *diagram* you.

3. A third method is to make a poster or collage out of magazine pictures that *illustrate* you and your life.

4. Make up your own idea for telling your life story.

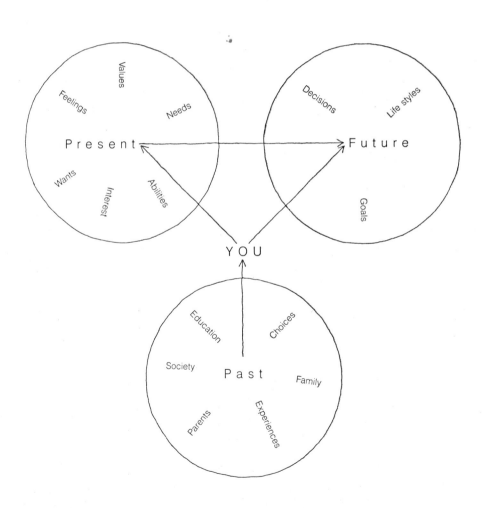

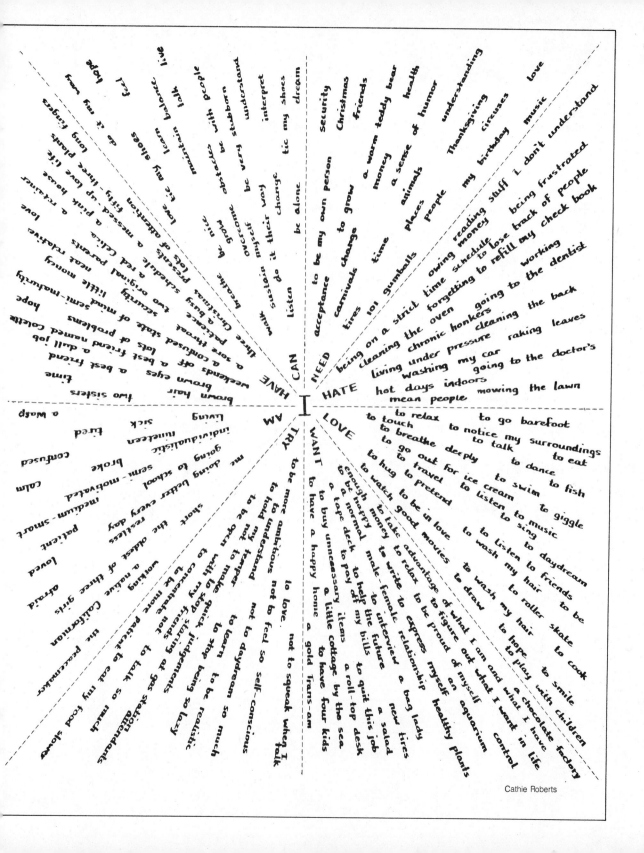

Cathie Roberts

E. Your accomplishments

Below, list things you feel good about having accomplished in your life. This is an important list. Keep it growing and enjoy it.

_____

_____

_____

_____

_____

_____

_____

_____

_____

_____

Six most satisfying accomplishments

1. _____

2. _____

3. _____

4. _____

5. _____

6. _____

Two   Roles and realities:

Sinking the stereotypes

U nderstanding your own needs, wants, and values is only the first step in choosing a career that can lead to personal growth. Next you need to examine the various roles people play. We all function in a variety of roles: mother, father, student, senior citizen, handicapped, minority, husband, wife, to name a few. When we discover a person's roles, we usually make assumptions based on stereotypes: we put the person in a box. Labeling saves time and energy, but it imposes limitations on our thinking. When you are making life choices, it's important to explore assumptions about various roles and decide whether those assumptions are correct. Beware of false generalizations: "Women can't handle engineering because they are poor in math."

To start, it may help you to explore the "American Dream," which involved roles in a way of life that was supposed to be achievable for the majority of people in this country in the years immediately following World War II. The dream has been a motivator for the life choices of many men and women.

The American Dream included a cozy house in the suburbs with a two-car garage and two healthy, bright children: an older boy and a younger girl. Father commuted to work in a proper suit and tie and worked hard supporting his family as a successful manager. His loving wife "did not work" but stayed at home, dusting up a bit, attending to child problems, preparing each day for her husband's return to their little nest. If she ever worked, it was at a "feminine" position (not engineering) and only temporarily, until she could entrust herself to the care of a man. Marriage meant "living happily ever after."

Until the mid-1960's, many couples had an opportunity to make the dream come true. (Of course, their chances were better if they were white, Anglo-Saxon, and Protestant.) But today, only about seven percent of the population resembles the idealized family described above. A large number of Americans live in cities. A great many are struggling to survive on very small incomes. Many have more

29

than two children, some have none. Many are unmarried, separated, divorced, widowed, remarried with various sets of children, his and hers.

Parenting is not pure bliss in a society beset with problems of permissiveness, sex, drugs, crime, and violence. It seems at times a thankless job to those who have made sacrifices for their children. Men and women are questioning their basic roles; some are swinging, swaying, and struggling to sort out their values. Women run away from home. Men become house-husbands and rear children. Many people—especially the elderly, the handicapped, and members of minorities—are poor and isolated from the mainstream of society.

Thus the American Dream which we had assumed was the "average American" way of life turns out to be the seven percent stereotype, and therefore a myth for most people. But many people still see this lifestyle as ideal and still believe that a great many Americans live this way. The media, especially television commercials, support this view despite real-life evidence to the contrary.

Old images, new imperatives

It is important to make career decisions based on reality, rather than on stereotypes about how people *should* live, what people *should* be, or how people *seem* to be. In reality, many people are choosing new directions, which they hope will turn out to be more in harmony with their needs and their individuality. In this chapter we will examine new directions chosen by people who are changing roles on a scale unheard of in previous generations. Your role as reader might involve evaluating these basic societal roles for yourself. First we will focus on the special problems faced by women. Next we will consider the male role and its growing pains. Then we will take a look at difficulties that minorities, handicapped, teenagers, and aging people meet in achieving their hopes and dreams, in creating a lifestyle that meets their needs.

True woman: dream of the future

At age 72 Elizabeth Cady Stanton said, speaking to the International Council of Women, "The younger women are starting with great advantages over us. They have the results of our experience; they have superior opportunities for education; they will find a more enlightened public sentiment for discussion; they will have more courage to take the rights which belong to them. . . . Thus far, women have been the mere echoes of men. Our laws and constitution, our creeds and codes, and the customs of social life are all of masculine origin. The true woman is as yet a dream of the future."[1]

Somehow that quotation sounds more recent than 1888! "The true woman is as yet a dream of the future." The *stereotypical, mythical* woman in the American

Dream was first a wife, next a mother, rarely herself as a woman. Her life was defined by the roles of others. She served their needs. The women's movement brought a general feeling to many that this model was not the "true woman." Certainly it did not describe *every* woman. Historically, about 20 percent of American women do not marry.

Today women are examining their roles, attempting to see themselves as individuals, trying to make choices. To examine those choices, we will begin with statistics released by the Women's Bureau of the Department of Labor in August 1978. Here are the facts about women working outside the home—women who don't fit the stereotype in the American Dream.

1. Ninety percent of all women work at some time in their lives. The average woman works for at least 23 years. Two-thirds work out of economic necessity: they are single, divorced, widowed, or married to men earning less than $10,000 a year. About 50 percent of women with working husbands also work, and the percentage is increasing.
2. The highest percentage of working women are in the age range of 18 to 24 and 35 to 54, that is, women very likely not involved with child rearing. The life expectancy of a female born in 1975 is 75 years. In 1920, it was 55 years; 33 percent of women with children under three years of age are now working.
3. Women with more education are more likely to work. Throughout her career, a woman with a college education can expect to earn as much as a male with an eighth grade education.
4. A woman earns three-fifths the salary of a male in an equivalent position, and this discrepancy is *increasing*. In this context, *Psychology Today*, in March 1975, described woman as "58 percent of a man."
5. The number of women in traditional male occupations has always been small. Now males in these occupations seem to be increasing their resistance to female entry. Women are concentrated more and more in less skilled, less rewarding, low-paying jobs. Women hold 14 percent of the often lucrative blue collar jobs in the country, only a 3.1 percent increase since 1960! There are women to be found in almost every traditionally male occupation—but not in significant numbers.
6. New job openings going to women are increasing (1 percent) while male employment is declining slightly (1 percent)—a worry to Senator Jacob Javits, who said Congress may have to act to preserve jobs for men!

Throughout our society, many people are still oblivious to the *real* status of women. In California, Pat Ackley administered a questionnaire on the above facts to a large group of educators and school counselors. Results of the Women and Work Questionnaire indicate that even these specialists are not aware of the facts.[2]

Family, career, or both?   Every person has to resolve questions that involve career vs. family. If a man travels and works nights, is he neglecting his family or only working hard to provide for their needs? Most people agree it's a question the man has to decide for himself. The same question applies to the woman who works outside the home—only in her case, the question is raised with uneasiness and disapproval.

In the small nuclear family of today, full-time child rearing can be expected to take only seven to ten years of a 75-year existence. If a woman remains at home until age 35 or 40, she still has 25 to 30 years to fill with some kind of activity before she reaches retirement age at 65. The nuclear family makes grandmothering a part-time job, if babysitting is needed at all. Grandmother and grandchildren may be living in widely separated geographic areas. Where once kids played and coffee flowed freely among friends, an empty nest in daytime-desolate suburbia may be the lot of the middle-class woman.

By this time, volunteering and playing bridge and golf has worn thin, and work involvement is felt as a compelling need. Women need work for the same reason men do: money and fulfillment. No one seems to doubt that men need work. Even the Kennedys and the Rockefellers work. We sympathize with men who are out of work more than a few months and with those in forced retirement, but we rarely feel concern for women in the same position.

Many husbands welcome the increased economic security that a wife's income provides. And many mothers are helping to pay their children's college expenses. But even if she is not one of the 66 percent who must work out of economic necessity, a woman needs to realize that there is some danger in turning over to another the complete responsibility for total economic support. Women need professional skills as insurance against a crisis, such as divorce or widowhood.

Women who are successful in their careers may well be happier wives and mothers than those who feel trapped at home. Many women who have chosen motherhood are exploring viable ways to do it well and still have successful careers. Some employers let women work part-time for a few years, share a job with another person, or act as consultants during the child-rearing period. Studies show increased productivity as a surprising result of this flexibility.

People are concerned that men will be pushed out of jobs if too many women come into the labor market and also that wages will fall. Barbara R. Bergman, speaking on the economics of the women's movement, estimates that if the forty-hour work week fell to thirty-one, all potential workers could be accommodated and end up with more leisure. She also adds that working women use more goods and services, not fewer, thus further increasing productivity.[3]

Many men appreciate their wives' sharing some of the economic burden of the family. They, in turn, are able to get more involved with life at home. Both partners in the relationship benefit from a more balanced lifestyle. Some men whose wives enjoy working are cutting down on their own work hours, again moving toward more balance.

Others feel threatened by the thought of a working wife. Long accustomed to seeing themselves as "sole provider," they see their main role in life eroding. But as Bess Meyerson says, "When it comes to machismo versus mouths to feed, machismo is a luxury no family can afford."[4] Self-fulfillment also may be a necessity, not a luxury, for some women.

Women should feel free to choose either full-time work or full-time motherhood without being pressured by the expectations of others. Society should value their contribution as important on every level.

Women don't have wives at home In most cases working wives and mothers can expect to carry the burden of household chores and child care. Alice Cook, Cornell Professor and scholar in residence at Stanford University's Center for Research on Women, surveyed nineteen nations, then published a report entitled "The Working Mother." She concluded, "The husband spends very little more time assisting the wife and mother with household tasks when she works outside the home than when she does not."[5] Younger and better educated couples are an exception, but not yet numerous enough to affect the statistics significantly.

Eve Steadman, a wife who returned to school, wrote this fantasy about men and housework:

> Women have always worked. The term "working women" usually indicates that these women are working for pay and that they have some choice about the kind of work they will perform. Many years ago, when I felt trapped in a future of endless diapers, dishes, and debris, I used to speculate about what would happen if the work situation pushed upon women were also applied to men. First of all, men could have no choice; every man by virtue of his biology would have exactly the same work. Second, this work would be comparable with that of women, that is, featuring monotony, drudgery, and repetition. Suppose, I thought, every man regardless of talents and interests were forced to be a ditchdigger. The man would not only dig all day, but every night while he slept someone would come by and push all the dirt back into the ditch! When he faced the dirt next morning, he would be expected to look glamorous and cheerful. Under these conditions, the Men's Revolution would not have been long in coming!

Studies generally show that females are socialized at an early age to reject high achievement in areas considered typically male and to discount their achievement in typically female activities. "I don't work. I'm just a housewife." Thus some women over-compensate for becoming career women by emphasizing "feminine appearance and behavior." Such nonassertive behavior can be self-defeating. If they also try to be the perfect housewife/mother, they may experience a physically and emotionally damaging way of living.[6]

But Caryl Rivers of Boston University is optimistic for the future of liberated marriage, which she defines as one in which there is rough parity of both "the dirt work and the glory."[7] Each woman—each couple—who is going to change from the traditional lifestyle will have to make adjustments. Some men have been strongly socialized to see housework as very unmasculine. But many people value a reasonably clean house and occasional home-cooked meals. The business of living, of maintaining oneself and one's home, is necessary, is hard work, and is not often perceived as stimulating.

Add babies—add more of the above. Who's to take care of it all if a wife works? A career woman doesn't have a housewife at home. This fact can become friction!

Child care   Along with household care, working mothers must be concerned with finding effective child care where there is supervision of play, learning, and social life. The child care must be reliable, especially if the mother is competing with men at work. Panic over babysitters is no help to the serious pursuit of a career, nor is worry over a sick or distressed child. A mother's need for leisure on weekends and holidays should be considered.

Men, long socialized to see child responsibility as someone else's problem, will often not "see" what needs to be done.

Communication with family/friends/colleagues   Women, especially those with mates and/or children, must be ready to communicate with everyone around them. Unless she is totally on her own, a woman's career decisions will affect others. They may be unwilling or unable to adapt to the changes she initiates.

Such sweeping innovations in traditional roles is a risk-taking procedure. Some relationships do not survive. A woman who wishes others to change is surprised to find that she must initiate changes in herself first. The result can be alienation or, with effort, a much more rewarding closeness.

Communication to *facilitate* intimacy rather than destroy it is a skill that can be learned. A time of decision is a good time to join a counseling group or get some individual help. Sorting out feelings and learning to share them in a caring way is important for personal growth. Many people's problems (maybe all?) stem from poor habits of sharing feelings. It may take skill and effort and risk and courage, going through tears and fears, but the results over time can be well worth it.

"Queen Bee"   Women must be prepared for the "Queen Bee Syndrome"— the prejudice they sometimes meet from women who have "made it" by their own hard work and who are loath to help others. Some women enjoy telling of their struggle and success, but are quick to add that "openings like this are no longer available." Sadly, some of these successful people are very critical of and impatient with those behind them. They have yet to learn what all self-actualizing people know:

The more you help others, the more successful you'll be.

New directions for men

While women are trying to define new roles, men also face dilemmas because their role is too rigidly defined. Society says that their careers are primary and their families secondary, so men have to keep on working until they are forced to retire. But we are becoming aware that many men reach a crisis in mid-life—a crisis that involves reevaluation of careers.

Much energy goes into the daily competition for success in the marketplace. Men who have "made it" have to work hard to "keep it." Often they come to a dead end where no more promotions are possible, and they have to relinquish their life ambitions. The same old job has become too familiar; all the challenge is gone. Like many women, many men feel trapped in monotonous, demanding, or demeaning jobs. Studs Terkel interviewed many male workers and found that the majority were dissatisfied with their work.[8]

Unfortunately, career success does not prevent the crisis. Some men achieve their long-sought goals only to ask, "Was it worth it?" Perhaps they have moved up into administration and now find themselves in prestigious positions that they do not enjoy. Sometimes these jobs involve long hours, trips away from home, and frequent moving. The result is alienation from the family—a loss of nurturing that can be critical, especially in times of crisis.

Whether equal to the task or not, men have had full economic responsibility for their families. Often they are expected to spend weekends and vacations doing heavy work at home, with little time for rest and recreation. As children grow older and require less care, a husband may resent a wife who stays home enjoying her leisure and playing cards with her friends. Enculturated to deny many human feelings, men are allowed to get angry, but not to show fears or tears. The successful man, as well as the unsuccessful, may be leading a life of "quiet desperation."

Yet the alternatives may seem frightening. Changing careers may mean stepping down, with a resulting loss of income and possibly a feeling of defeat. Instead of retraining for a new line of work, the dissatisfied working man will probably decide to "stick it out" until retirement or to look for a new company with a fresh outlook. He seems to have fewer choices than his wife, who can change her life dramatically by going back to college or taking a job outside the home. For both husband and wife, in most instances, the immediate goal is not self-actualization, but paying off the mortgage, educating the children, and possibly helping the elderly grandparents.

Mid-life is a crucial time, a time to realize that *dis*-illusionment means seeing more clearly. It is a time to re-order values, build confidence, face areas of deficiency, and develop neglected segments of one's life. Mid-life can be a healing time, a time for growth, the time to befriend oneself by putting one's world into perspective—a time to ask, "What do I really want out of life?"

As they face the issues and *grow* through this crisis, some men develop a new, deeper, more mature outlook that restores their energy and vitality. Some are amazed to learn that they need better skills in human relations and communications, instead of a new job or a new kind of work. Some find the courage to make needed changes in work or home life, go back to school, break out of old patterns. The need to let go of the past is a common human experience that can bring us closer to the real meaning of life. Both men and women need support when they are experiencing these critical periods in the normal course of human development.

✳ ✳ ✳ ✳ ✳ ✳ ✳ ✳ ✳ ✳ ✳ ✳

D O N ' T   L E T   L I F E
discourage you;
everyone who got where he is
had to begin where he was.
—RICHARD L. EVANS

✳ ✳ ✳ ✳ ✳ ✳ ✳ ✳ ✳ ✳ ✳ ✳

Teenagers and young adults

Teenagers who have done well in high school are usually confident and college-bound—but they are *not* the majority. Many of their peers have not yet learned necessary survival skills or experienced any feeling of achievement. They lack both the job skills and the sophistication that are needed to find work in a tight job market. Their sagging self-image is not improved when they are rejected by prospective employers who have neither the time nor the budget to train raw recruits.

Today business and industry are engaged in myriad mysterious machinations that challenge the understanding of even the brightest adult. No wonder that young people, fresh out of senior government class, are lost! Some high schools acknowledge students' needs by offering work experience and career observation and exploration programs. Often the shyest, least successful students will not even apply. For many, approaching the first rung of the career ladder is the most difficult step in the entire lifetime career process. Statistics show that the unemployment rate for young adults is two to three times higher than the rate for the remainder of the population.

The aging

Opportunities for rewarding work become fewer for both men and women as they grow older. Those over forty who have experienced job hunting can attest to that.

Many stay at jobs they've outgrown rather than face possible rejection. Our youth-oriented, throw-away culture sees little value in the older person. So we have, in Lillian Hellman's words, "the wisdom that comes with age that we can't make use of."[9]

The numbers of lonely aged living on meager money are growing. Inflation and taxes gnaw away at their fixed incomes. Crime frightens some of them into isolation. Lack of opportunity to contribute causes a sense of uselessness, which, in turn, causes some to give up.

Older women returning to the job market from the housewife role are in double jeopardy. Here "sexism meets ageism" according to Tish Sommers, Coordinator of NOW's Task Force on Older Women:

> Sexism is compounded as a woman grows older. Jobs are harder to come by; the dependency status increases; self-image deteriorates; health care goes from bad to worse; marriages flounder. For a large majority of older women, poverty is no longer on the doorstep—it moves in. Our society is not only permeated with sexism from top to bottom, it is also pervaded with ageism. This denial of personhood affects both genders, but women, already weakened by sexism, are especially vulnerable.[10]

Many employers recognize that the mature person can bring a great deal of stability and responsibility to a position. One doesn't lose ability and experience on the eve of one's 65th birthday any more than one grows up fully at age 21.

Minorities

Minorities also are caught in the stereotype bind. Many cluster in ghettoes, struggling just to stay even. Their expectations are low because, among the poor, young people rarely get a chance to observe adult role models in successful positions.

Like the Queen Bee, some minority people who have moved up also move away from those they might help. The young are left to find themselves, often in a hostile environment. Add the frustration of "others" making decisions that affect them and getting what seems like a large share of affluence, and the future may seem hopeless. Among minority youth in cities, the unemployment rate is 40 percent. Many are unable to begin careers because opportunities are limited or withheld.

Persons with handicaps

Society has never been successful at dealing with persons who are disabled. A silent minority, too, they were expected to stay in their place, which was one of low expectations. They have often struggled with a poor self-image and feelings of hopelessness about even making a living, much less a contribution to society.

In the present climate of focus on individual rights, such groups are asking for rightful recognition of the skills they possess. They are demanding more access to government, business, industry, education, and all phases of life. Society is forced to take note that here are people able to make a living and to make valuable contributions.

The economic perspective

Counselor Veronese Anderson sees society with mainly the white, affluent, successful male at the top and his family with him by association. At the lower levels are those of poor to modest incomes: minorities exist at these levels in percentages far out of proportion to their numbers.[11] As the levels rise, the numbers diminish. It can be seen as a socioeconomic tower.

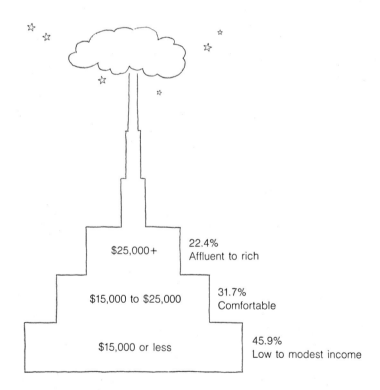

United States–All families: 1977 income distribution*

*Source: U.S. Department of Commerce, Bureau of the Census, *Statistical Abstract of the United States: 1978*, p. 452.

Some people see discrimination against women and other groups as part of capitalistic planning. As Marilyn Power Goldberg points out, we need a "marginal workforce to smooth over cycles in the economy and to perform vital but menial and poorly paid jobs. We need to keep reinforcing their image of inferiority."[12]

John Kenneth Galbraith also sees society using the concept of the "convenient social virtue" to keep women (and again, various minorities) in a position of free service.

> "The convenient social virtue" ascribes merit to any pattern of behavior, however uncomfortable or unnatural for the individual involved, that serves the comfort or well-being of the more powerful members of the community.

> The nurse, the teacher, the nun, the community volunteer, the "cheerful, dutiful draftee": all have accepted social approval instead of pay. The economy benefits from free service. Galbraith sees the cheerful housewife of the nuclear family, who takes pride in her virtue as provider of goods, as the "consumer par excellence," another advantage to the economy.[13]

Changing attitudes

Everyone wants access to a more enriched life. In response to human needs, attitudes are slowly changing. Perhaps most Americans now agree—in theory, if not in practice—that no one should be denied self-fulfillment because of sex, creed, color, handicaps, or age.

After two decades of consciousness raising, changes are in the air everywhere. When her husband, Daniel, was ambassador to India, Liz Moynihan said: "I'd go to parties if the State Department paid me. But I don't believe in their getting two for the price of one."

Nontraditional lifestyles become more prevalent as people choose *careers* that are important to them. When a wife has a chance to move up and hence away, some couples are opting for commuting to marriage on weekends. One San Francisco banking executive plans to spend six months there and six months in New York where her husband and bank headquarters reside!

Some husbands are giving up their jobs and moving up, up, and away with their wives; some are opting for house-husband roles. Caryl Rivers asks, "Can a woman be both liberated and married? And a parent? Can a man? These are the questions being asked these days."

Minorities are moving up, becoming more visible in every area of life. Persons with handicaps are wheeling and whizzing out of isolation and assertively speaking up about their needs. The elderly are beginning to feel a sense of energy and ability to change their lot in life.

As you saw in Chapter 1, growing as a person means changing, adjusting to both inner and outer reality. It means expansion into new and exciting areas of life. Stereotypes about how we *should* be keep us from becoming what we *could* be.

It seems that in our society we have come to a time of decision about how we want to be. More aware of our fragile environment, our energy shortage, our waste of resources, we know that we can't "have it all." But a further look at our needs, wants, and values might show us that we can have more than enough. It can be a good time for us if we act wisely, giving all of us a chance to develop more balanced lives and to free ourselves from stereotypes. To paraphrase Elizabeth Cady Stanton, "The true person is as yet a dream of the future." Let's hope that future is not too distant.

EXERCISES: ROLES

1. Form a triad to discuss problems of the following people.

A. First women you know, and then men, who fit these descriptions:

1. Have never worked in jobs for pay
2. Have always worked in jobs for pay
3. Have worked part-time or temporarily
4. Are their own sole support
5. Support a family
6. Are in traditional jobs
7. Are in nontraditional jobs

B. Minority, handicapped, and elderly people you know, who fit these descriptions:

1. Are/are not in status positions
2. Have/have not overcome barriers to the mainstream
3. Are leading an energetic, fulfilled life or are discouraged and defeated
4. Are doing unique, creative things

C. Teenagers and young adults entering the job market.

D. Talk about stereotypes.

1. What are the various roles you play in life?
2. What is expected of you in each of these roles?
3. Do you live your roles as you choose, or as others expect you to?

2. Discuss in class or write your answers on a separate sheet of paper:

   A. What have you learned from this chapter?

   B. What stereotypes and prejudices would you like to change in yourself and in society?

Three — Career dimensions:

Scanning the subtleties

We are gathering information to match a special person—you—with satisfying positions in the world of work. In order to match your needs, wants, and values with job specifications, you should examine various dimensions of career choice, including some that are often overlooked. When you finally enter the workplace, you may have to make some compromises, but the ideal is to minimize the compromises and maximize the match.

The search has different stages. For many people, the journey begins at ground zero with not an idea in sight. But as you gather career information, you reach a mid-point where you seem to be engulfed in too many ideas. In other words, things seem to get worse before they get better. When that happens, it's essential that you begin to lighten the burden by choosing. You simply can't follow every career in one lifetime. The calmer you stay, the more easily you will arrive at your decision point.

Next, consider the extent of your commitment. Do you want a career or just a job? A job might be defined as something one does to earn money with little involvement beyond one's physical/mental presence performing in a routine way. Many people at all levels of intelligence and creativity use work in this way: some because this is the only work they want or can get; others to support hobbies and creative activities for which there seem to be no work opportunities.

A career can be seen as a series of work experiences that represent a progression in a field. It is work that captivates more of one's total energy. A career is something planned for, trained for, involving dedication of time and talent beyond the minimum required.

When two people are doing identical work, one may view it as "just a job" and another as "my career." Sometimes a person trains and sacrifices to achieve a career only to face disillusion for some unforeseen reason and end up performing tasks mechanically, seeing no way out. Conversely, some people have

43

Career choice continuum

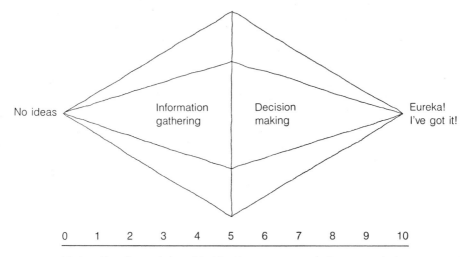

No ideas

Information gathering

Decision making

Eureka! I've got it!

0   1   2   3   4   5   6   7   8   9   10

Mark an X on the scale from 0 to 10 where you are *now* in the career choice continuum.

been known to perform what society calls "menial" work with a level of dedication worthy of a professional.

Some work is almost impossible to do without a great deal of personal involvement. In our society, for example, "moving up" generally is an all-consuming activity. How much are you willing to sacrifice? For some, "success" has meant loss of family, health, friendship, and leisure. One can get caught up in work only to find that other values have slipped away.

Others can pursue a career with great dedication and yet keep a balance. How much involvement is enough for you? Sometimes your commitment to a career increases greatly when you become aware of your interests and skills and the way they relate to the world of work. Motivation and energy soar. Keep the question of commitment in mind as you consider your career choice.

Areas of interest: The personality mosaic

A major decision point is that of interest area. Where do you, with all the unique facets of your personality, feel most comfortable? The human personality can be likened to a stained glass window—a mosaic of light and color.

A stained glass window is a very concrete, permanent thing of carefully chosen colors. Yet it changes with the changing sun. In darkness it is almost nothing compared to its brilliance in the light.

> *It takes*
>
> > *its life from light*
> > *it sleeps at night*
> > *and comes ablaze at dawn*
> > > *it holds the day*
> > > *'til shadows fade*
> > > *its brilliance strangely gone.*

Analogously, the human personality can be seen as a mosaic of six major themes: realistic, investigative, artistic, social, enterprising, and conventional. John Holland believes that one of these is usually a dominant orientation that plays a highly important role in career choice. It is probably not possible for most of us to deal with many areas of interest. We become preoccupied with a certain one early in life. It becomes our main thrust, largely because of value choices that stem from our needs and wants.[1]

But new "lights" appear and can be developed if we are open to them. Sometimes it means a whole new direction, sometimes a creative blend or "mix" of old and new. Discovering our predominant component can be a help in career choice. Being aware of our "lesser lights" can also shed some illumination and enrichment. Personal growth leads to the discovery of new dimensions in ourselves. We are all born with innumerable possibilities. Some talents remain undeveloped for half a lifetime, then surface in time to bring joy to our middle and senior years.

Perhaps, too, we can see as an ideal the "universal person" of the Renaissance: able to be all things with apparently equal ease, at home in all settings and with all people, truly self-actualized.

The career ladder: How far up?

People function in the workplace at various levels. Perhaps your interests can be matched to one of the levels in the career ladder on page 46. The chart identifies four levels that can be found in many institutional work settings. In some settings, such as the military, the structure is very rigid. In others the levels are less formal and less evident. As you climb the ladder, more education is needed for each level of responsibility. See where you fit in and where you would like to go.

All workplaces, whether a lawyer's office, a large catering service, a hospital, or an international manufacturing corporation, have similar structures.

A very small staff consists of the boss, who has many management functions,

The Career Ladder

Position	Responsibility	Education	Support staff
	Top level		
Top management and professionals, such as Presidents Board members Doctors Lawyers	The decision-makers, who are responsible for nearly everything. There is more independence at this level.	Ph.D., D.D., M.D., M.B.A., etc. Technical and professional expertise	Operates at all levels to provide auxiliary services, such as Personnel Accounting Communications Research Purchasing Marketing Data Processing Secretarial Maintenance
	Middle level		
Middle management and professionals, such as Department heads Engineers Nurses Teachers	Shares responsibility with the top level and enjoys some independence.	M.A., M.B.A., M.S., B.S., B.A., etc. Middle-level expertise	
	Lower level		
Lower management and technicians, such as Supervisors Lead persons Legal assistants LVNs	Responsible for a small part of decision-making. May supervise others.	A.A., A.S., vocational, or on-the-job training	
	The workers		
Basic production and service work, such as Trades, crafts Assemblers Machinists Waiters/waitresses	Responsible for a particular function. Entry level jobs, often repetitive work.	High school, apprenticeship. Usually *some* training or experience is needed.	

and one assistant who does the rest. Some places "contract out" certain jobs like data processing, accounting, income tax, and maintenance service. As more work- ers are added to the staff, specialization increases.

The fewer the workers, the more likely each worker will have more interesting and varied work with more responsibility. A medical assistant in a doctor's office may do billing, typing, a little family counseling, public relations, tax work, and research and never know what each day will bring. In a larger place, entry-level workers can expect to do a more limiting job, whether it is putting lettuce leaves on a thousand sandwiches, or soldering a link in a thousand electronic circuits, or typing a thousand letters.

So size and complexity of the workplace can be a very important factor in job choice. In a larger place a specific position may be subject to more limitations; however, possibilities for change, including moving both over and up, are greater. In a smaller place work may be more varied and responsibility greater, but options are narrowed.

Where do you fit in this scheme of things? How far up the ladder do you wish to be? (It is lonely at the top but exciting and challenging. It is comfy at the bottom but often not so rich or interesting!) If you know where you want to be a few years from now, you will not limit yourself by neglecting present opportunities.

Usually education and training increase as the level of involvement increases, but we have all heard of the self-made man (and now the self-made woman).

Lifestyle—another decision point

Lifestyles range from the very conservative to the 'way-out radical. A conservative lifestyle might be defined as "typical" and very proper, like the 7 percent stereotype in Chapter 2.

Most people deviate from that conservative style to a moderate degree. Neighbors and friends may raise their eyebrows a bit at some out-of-the-ordinary choices, but usually they get used to them and accept them. For example, it's becoming common for married couples to postpone parenting, often to the chagrin of grandparents-to-be. The extreme end of the spectrum would be a lifestyle based on choices that are highly unusual and controversial. Some parents experience great distress when their children choose affiliation with extremely radical political groups or religious cults.

Attitudes about lifestyles vary from time to time and from place to place. What shocked Grandma might not turn a head today. Lifestyles that pass unnoticed in the cities might become the talk of the town in a semirural community. When you pick your starting point, remember that lifestyle changes may occur as a result of career choice. Lifestyle involves a whole complex of manifestations—housing, style of dress, social life, recreation, education, transportation, religious preference— with implications far beyond the confines of the workplace. In short, our lifestyle reflects our most cherished values.

Work and its consequent lifestyle are bound up tightly with self-image, ego, and status. Sometimes Americans place undue emphasis on "what a person does" for a living. We try to fit each worker into a stereotype. Archie Bunker owns a tavern— he is not a hair stylist! Archie watchs sports on TV, drinks beer with the boys, rides the subway. He does not go to the opera, play the violin, or drive a Porsche. (I know of a railroad engineer who played the organ at church, never swore, and attended the symphony regularly with his wife. His co-workers had trouble relating to him. They called him "Molly.") Some people find it difficult to relate to any new acquaintance until they find out what he or she does for a living. That information then screens out any new input that doesn't fit a stereotype.

The point is that a job can change you. You will learn new skills—technical skills, social skills, and tricks of the trade. Your career choice can lead to new involvements, new values, and even new ways of seeing yourself.[2]

THE NOW SOCIETY

Very pleased to meet you. What does your husband do?

Universal Press Syndicate,
Copyright 1978

Examining skills

Usually your interests are a clue to your skills. Most people acquire skills in areas they enjoy and tend to neglect other areas. If you like something, you spend time getting better at it . . . and like it more . . . and spend more time . . .

Skills are a measure of the effectiveness with which our minds and bodies manage in the world around us. They also deal with the way we manage ourselves. We are born already well equipped with certain skills that enable us at once to begin using our bodies and our senses to recognize, interpret, acquire, and accomplish many things. Look at any six-*month*-old and be amazed at the complexity of acquired skills. Then compare with a six-*year*-old and be further astounded.

Our minds and bodies possess mental and physical skills with emotions somehow permeating the two and affecting social relationships. Using these powers, we deal with only three areas:

Data—A human mind can take in great quantities of information, or data, in the form of words, numbers, and symbols. All day long the mind processes these data in a variety of ways, expressing complex thoughts and ideas often creatively, and always in a way unique to the individual.

Things—Skills of the human body depend on its degree of strength, agility, and coordination in relating to other physical objects. The way the body fixes, builds, and plans things often verges on the creative, as in architecture.

People—Those abilities which determine how well we get along with other humans involve all sorts of body/mind perceptions and linguistic skills. The emotions, which are physical responses to sensory information, permeate our mental processes and influence our behavior and relationships with others.

Our skills with data, people, and things work together in a blend of mental/physical abilities, emotionally expressed in creating music, art, and literature and also in scientific and technical works. But stop and think: every day, using your mind, body, and emotions, *you* create your life.

We can divide the human person into mind, body, and emotions only as a mental exercise. Philosophers have struggled through the centuries to understand these everyday terms. Because of our culture's emphasis on education as an intellectual exercise, we have glorified so-called mental abilities to the neglect of other areas. We say that someone works well with his/her hands as if to imply that while this work is being done, nothing is going on in his/her head. However, the mind must attend to the learning of even the simplest tasks, although it seems to disengage itself once habit takes over.

Mind/body skills can also be used for personal management. They enable you to adapt to a variety of environments and manage certain factors: yourself (appearance and manner, impulses and feelings, needs and wants); people (those in authority, your peers and subordinates); things (materials and property); and data (time, space, information, and ideas).

Do you manage yourself responsibly, creatively, and with initiative? Basically, the question is, are you part of the problem or part of the solution? Do you hinder or help the situation called *work*?

One ability that relates to all the others is "common sense," which is how we deal with "the business of living." Physical, mental, emotional, social, and financial well-being depend upon this ability in large measure. You have survived modern life thus far. You must possess a good measure of skills in *all* areas.

These skills dealing with data, people, and things can be seen in terms of their "transferability." If we have good mental and physical skills, they can be used in a variety of situations. It is comforting to note that the majority of jobs require only average skills. But most people think of the specific and learned skills of highly trained persons like surgeons and opera singers, and groan at their own "lack of talent." They fail to recognize the talents they've been using effectively for years.

For example, "just a housewife" is manager of a complex organization, and she deals with the three all-encompassing areas of data, people, and things. Some management personnel realize that housewives have acquired many useful skills. Ray Killian says, "Women might have limited business experience, but many of them offset this with management experience in the home. They have managed family finances, solved problems, and made decisions. They have learned to economize, to save time by developing efficient methods, and to maintain harmony. . . . Much of this experience can be transferred to their jobs and to supervisory roles."[3]

Estell Buchanan, a Colorado management consultant, feels that women are "psychologically attuned to the new concept of business team leadership." Socialized to be skilled in communications, empathy, human relations, and understanding, women can be unusually effective in modern decentralized organizations. "The old concept of a boss in absolute command over his area is yielding: that is masculine and outdated."[4]

So it is not a question of whether you have skills. Rather, of all the skills you possess, which do you *enjoy* using? And more important, which would you like to use in a *work setting*? What skills are you motivated to acquire and improve to get where you would like to be? In what ways would you like to narrow down your transferable data, people, things skills to work-specific skills? For example, with good finger dexterity, would you prefer to become adept at the guitar, the typewriter, or both?

Many jobs require more transferable skills and personal skills (the kind you have already) than work-specific skills. Some jobs, of course, require further education and training in the work-specific skills. The time needed to get ready to do a particular job is an important consideration in career choice.

The work environment

Following your skills and interests may lead you into work environments that range from serene to frenetic. As a writer, for example, you might find yourself either researching in a library or risking your life as a war correspondent. The work environment, then, is another dimension that should be considered as you choose your career. There are many things you thoroughly enjoy but might hate if you had to do them

- under pressure
- a thousand times a day
- in a hot, crowded, noisy, and otherwise unpleasant place
- for an irritable boss with ulcers

I enjoy cooking, but I'm fairly certain I would not enjoy serving a million hamburgers at McDonald's. I would not like cooking regularly for any large group, even in the most elegant setting. If I chose cooking as a career, I could consider some alternatives:

- teaching what I know to small groups of children or adults, perhaps at home or in a neighborhood center
- serving meals to small groups on special occasions; serving the elderly in neighborhoods, Meals on Wheels, catered breakfasts, luncheons, or dinners
- selling to a restaurant a special bread or dessert, or selling birthday and wedding cakes
- arranging wedding receptions, birthday parties, or business luncheons

To avoid making the wrong choice, try to get a little experience in the work environment—even if you have to volunteer—before investing a great deal of time, energy, and money in training. A young person who "loves animals" may find working at the local vet's office an exciting experience or that dealing with sick animals and worried owners is traumatic. On the other hand, every job will gradually (or quickly) demonstrate some unpleasant aspects. Basically, work is often *hard* work. One must function within the economic and time parameters of an organization. As Ben Franklin said, "Time is money." When both these items are in short supply, deadlines and shortages create pressure.

Human relations can require much of your energy as you seek to accommodate to the various personalities you meet at work. Sometimes a change in yourself can make a vast difference. You can learn to communicate more effectively, assert yourself in a tactful way, grow in self-confidence, become more considerate and understanding of the problems of others. It will usually be necessary to strike a balance: not make a "federal case" out of every annoyance, yet be able to make changes in a situation that clashes sharply with your sensibilities.

Sometimes asking for a change of work can alter your outlook. For example, could you answer questions at the information window part of the time instead of answering the phone all day? A change to another department or to a slightly different job often means a new start. You might learn to manage time or the flow of work activities in a more efficient manner.

Another subtlety of the workplace is its degree of sensitivity to personal needs. In today's world, the "business of living" is becoming increasingly complex. This term refers to the endless, and absolutely necessary, tasks each person must perform in regard to: (1) financial matters, such as banking, taxes, insurance, real estate, and other investments; (2) medical/dental care; (3) personal care, including food, clothing, and shelter; (4) child care in all of these categories; and (5) education—"keeping up with your field."

Some large corporations have begun to hire people to assist workers with these problems. For instance, some places have doctors or nurses for short-term consultation, financial services such as savings and loans, courses for work improvement, and even increased recreational activities. Some companies are finding that "flextime" is cutting down absenteeism and raising productivity when workers can arrange their own hours to take care of personal business needs.

Irving Goffman wrote in *Asylums* that just by reason of sheer numbers, institutions tend to become dehumanizing.[5] But large size doesn't always connote depersonalization. Within many a large organization, one can discover small, cohesive, caring groups of people looking out for each other's interests. This kind of support would not be found in a small place run by a tyrannical leader.

Barbara Garson studied three workplaces in New York. She reported that Fair Plan Insurance Company and Reader's Digest showed extremely restrictive policies for workers: no talking to other employees while working, no personal phone calls

HERMAN *by Unger*

Well, well, my secret file tells me that since 1948 this is your grandmother's seventh funeral.

Copyright 1977
Universal Press Syndicate

about family emergencies, and other rigid rules. In contrast, the report described the accounting office of a community college where five older women worked very hard to complete their tasks but managed to fit in noon parties, trips to the hospital to visit sick family members, and other personal ventures. No want ad or job description will ever deal with these "fringe benefits."[6]

How important are these things for you? Single parents, especially, carry burdens that demand attention not always amenable to an 8 to 5 schedule. One woman engineer noticed several male colleagues consulting on what she assumed was their project. On closer inspection, she found these newly divorced males discussing the merits of the crockpot for the working parent.

Sometimes the interpersonal characteristics of a job can change. One newly divorced mother enjoyed working in a small savings and loan office. An older woman gave her much understanding; the boss was great, and the younger workers a delight. But the boss, who had decided to work harder at "moving up," began to be more restrictive, even to the point of pressuring workers to stay overtime without pay. The older woman was being "phased out" as the company had decided to hire a "security guard/teller." The work atmosphere of the job changed from fun to funk. (The latest word from this office is that it's back to fun again: The now experienced working mother has become the manager.)

No matter how carefully you plan your career, at some time you are likely to have a job that does not meet your needs, supply more than a few of your wants,

HERMAN *by Unger*

"Night work! You mean when it's dark?"

Are you just drifting?
Start gathering information
about careers.

Are you swamped with
information?
It's time to start narrowing
the choices.

Stay calm, stay on course,
and you'll reach your
destination.

or represent your values. Then it is time for a change. You may decide to look for another job doing the same kind of work, or you may want to change fields entirely. When choosing a career, it is important to remember that all decisions have limitations. Being open and flexible can help you along the way. Don't feel that all choices are final.

By now, you've begun to think about various aspects of the career choice, such as career area, lifestyle, the career ladder, and your commitment to a career, rather than just a job. You're approaching the midpoint in the career choice continuum, and you're almost ready to begin "zeroing in" on the choice. Where are you now on the journey along the Career Choice Continuum?

EXERCISES: CAREERS

A. Quickly mark each statement *true* or *false*. Then discuss these issues in a small group.

_____ 1. Your interests are a blend of your needs, wants, and values.

_____ 2. The trick in selecting an occupation is to maximize the compromises and minimize the match.

_____ 3. A job is defined as a series of work experiences that represent a progression in a field.

_____ 4. In a job that requires a great deal of personal involvement, you may have to ask yourself, "How much am I willing to sacrifice?"

_____ 5. The fewer the workers in a job setting, the more likely each worker will find interesting and varied work with increasing responsibility.

_____ 6. Your self-image changes when you learn a new job activity.

_____ 7. Most people acquire skills in work that they enjoy and enjoy work in which they have developed skills.

_____ 8. The ability to deal with words, numbers, and other symbols of varying complexity reflects your _mental_ skills.

_____ 9. We frequently say that someone "works well with her hands" as if to imply that nothing is going on in her head.

_____ 10. A person who has common sense in most aspects of life is "skilled in the business of living."

B. Multiple choice: circle the letter that identifies the correct answer.

1. A job might be defined as:
   a. something one does to earn money, with little personal involvement
   b. a means to support hobbies and creative activities for which there seem to be no work opportunities
   c. both _a_ and _b_
   d. neither _a_ nor _b_

2. A career might be defined as:
   a. series of work experiences that represent a progression in a field
   b. work that captivates more of one's total energy
   c. work involving more dedication of time and talent than is minimally required
   d. all of the above

3. Which of the following would be components of lifestyle?
   a. education
   b. recreation
   c. transportation
   d. religious preference
   e. all of the above

4. We can analyze our _skill_ development in terms of:
   a. self-management abilities
   b. transferable abilities
   c. work-specific abilities
   d. interests
   e. successes
   f. any of the above

5. Since most jobs involve human relations, it is to your advantage to:
   a. communicate more effectively
   b. assert yourself in a tactful way
   c. grow in self-confidence
   d. become more considerate and understanding of the problems of others
   e. develop all of the above

6. One of the difficulties of living in today's complex world is having to deal with the multiplicity of decisions concerning:
   a. financial matters
   b. medical/dental care
   c. personal care
   d. child care
   e. one's personal education
   f. all of the above

C. A household is a workplace, too. Discuss the following:

   1. Name the goods and services your household provides to its members.
   2. In your household, who takes care of the following functions: management, finance/accounting, secretarial, maintenance, communications, purchasing?
   3. Do computers supply any services to your household? (Check your bank statement, water bill, charge statements.)
   4. In the workplace, the personnel department handles labor problems. How is the labor handled and divided in your household? Who settles labor disputes?
   5. What is your "commitment" to your household? Is it "just a job" or is it a "career"? (In other words, just a place to stay, or a very important place where you invest much of yourself to "make it work"?)
   6. What functions do you prefer in your household?
   7. Are there any chances for change/advancement?
   8. How long do you plan to stay with your present functions?
   9. Does the present lifestyle of your household meet your needs?
   10. Name some skills you use in these household functions. Which do you enjoy using?
   11. Describe the emotional climate of your household.
   12. Describe the physical appearance of your household.

Four — Finding your job satisfiers:

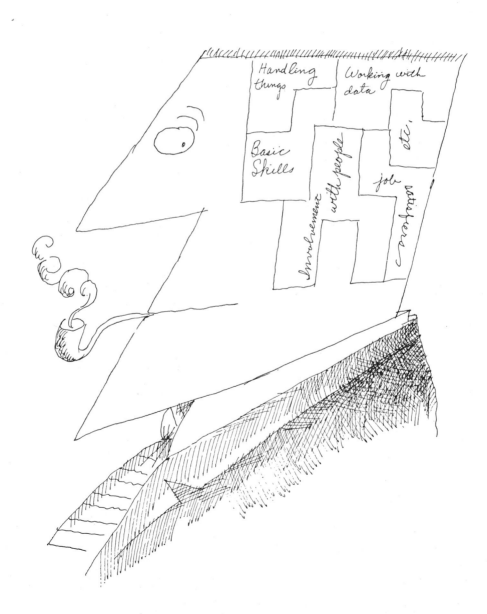

Self-assessment inventories

In this chapter you will take a series of self-assessment inventories: (1) the Personality Mosaic, (2) the Data /People /Things Involvement Indicator, (3) the Work Qualities Inventory, and (4) the Activities Analysis. Using the information from these exercises and the Job Group Chart, you will be able to zero in on which of 20,000 occupations match *you* and provide your satisfiers.

Try to respond as much by *feeling* your answers as by *thinking* them out. The results of these inventories depend on self-awareness. They are designed not to tell you about yourself, but to encourage you to think about the qualities you possess. Use pencil for all inventories so that you can go back and revise.

Don't imagine that you will immediately be ready for the ultimate career decision once these inventories are completed. Look at them instead as the first round of serious investigation. The results will then need to be sharpened, refined, and pinpointed. This sort of information about self isn't absorbed instantly. Like good coffee, it needs time to percolate.

Take the Personality Mosaic on the following pages, before you read anything else in this section.

EXERCISE

Personality Mosaic

Directions: Circle the numbers of statements that clearly feel like something you might say or do or think—something that feels like *you*.

1. It's important for me to have a strong, agile body.
2. I need to understand things thoroughly.
3. Music, color, beauty of any kind can really affect my moods.
4. People enrich my life and give it meaning.
5. I have confidence in myself that I can make things happen.
6. I appreciate clear directions so I know exactly what to do.
7. I can usually carry/build/fix things myself.
8. I can get absorbed for hours in thinking something out.
9. I appreciate beautiful surroundings; color and design mean a lot to me.
10. I love company.
11. I enjoy competing.
12. I need to get my surroundings in order before I start a project.
13. I enjoy making things with my hands.
14. It's satisfying to explore new ideas.
15. I always seem to be looking for new ways to express my creativity.
16. I value being able to share personal concerns with people.
17. Being a key person in a group is very satisfying to me.
18. I take pride in being very careful about all the details of my work.
19. I don't mind getting my hands dirty.
20. I see education as a lifelong process of developing and sharpening my mind.

21. I love to dress in unusual ways, to try new colors and styles.
22. I can often sense when a person needs to talk to someone.
23. I enjoy getting people organized and on the move.
24. A good routine helps me get the job done.
25. I like to buy sensible things I can make or work on myself.
26. Sometimes I can sit for long periods of time and work on puzzles or read or just think about life.
27. I have a great imagination.
28. It makes me feel good to take care of people.
29. I like to have people rely on me to get the job done.
30. I'm satisfied knowing that I've done an assignment carefully and completely.
31. I'd rather be on my own doing practical, hands-on activities.
32. I'm eager to read about any subject that arouses my curiosity.
33. I love to try creative new ideas.
34. If I have a problem with someone, I prefer to talk it out and resolve it.
35. To be successful, it's important to aim high.
36. I prefer being in a position where I don't have to take responsibility for decisions.
37. I don't enjoy spending a lot of time discussing things. What's right is right.
38. I need to analyze a problem pretty thoroughly before I act on it.
39. I like to rearrange my surroundings to make them unique and different.
40. When I feel down, I find a friend to talk to.
41. After I suggest a plan, I prefer to let others take care of the details.
42. I'm usually content where I am.
43. It's invigorating to do things outdoors.
44. I keep asking "why."
45. I like my work to be an expression of my moods and feelings.
46. I like to find ways to help people care more for each other.
47. It's exciting to take part in important decisions.
48. I'm always glad to have someone else take charge.
49. I like my surroundings to be plain and practical.
50. I need to stay with a problem until I figure out an answer.
51. The beauty of nature touches something deep inside me.
52. Close relationships are important to me.
53. Promotion and advancement are important to me.
54. Efficiency, for me, means doing a set amount carefully each day.
55. A strong system of law and order is important to prevent chaos.

56. Thought-provoking books always broaden my perspective.
57. I look forward to seeing art shows, plays, and good films.
58. I haven't seen you for so long; I'd love to know how you're doing.
59. It's exciting to influence people.
60. When I say I'll do it, I follow through on every detail.
61. Good, hard physical work never hurt anyone.
62. I'd like to learn all there is to know about subjects that interest me.
63. I don't want to be like everyone else; I like to do things differently.
64. Tell me how I can help you.
65. I'm willing to take some risks to get ahead.
66. I like exact directions and clear rules when I start something new.
67. The first thing I look for in a car is a well-built engine.
68. Those people are intellectually stimulating.
69. When I'm creating, I tend to let everything else go.
70. I feel concerned that so many people in our society need help.
71. It's fun to get ideas across to people.
72. I hate it when they keep changing the system just when I get it down.
73. I usually know how to take care of things in an emergency.
74. Just reading about those new discoveries is exciting.
75. I like to create happenings.
76. I often go out of my way to pay attention to people who seem lonely and friendless.
77. I love to bargain.
78. I don't like to do things unless I'm sure they're approved.
79. Sports are important in building strong bodies.
80. I've always been curious about the way nature works.
81. It's fun to be in a mood to try or do something unusual.
82. I believe that people are basically good.
83. If I don't make it the first time, I usually bounce back with energy and enthusiasm.
84. I appreciate knowing exactly what people expect of me.
85. I like to take things apart to see if I can fix them.
86. Don't get excited. We can think it out and plan the right move logically.
87. It would be hard to imagine my life without beauty around me.
88. People often seem to tell me their problems.
89. I can usually connect with people who get me in touch with a network of resources.
90. I don't need much to be happy.

Scoring your answers

To score, circle the same numbers below that you circled on the Personality Mosaic.

R	I	A	S	E	C
1	2	3	4	5	6
7	8	9	10	11	12
13	14	15	16	17	18
19	20	21	22	23	24
25	26	27	28	29	30
31	32	33	34	35	36
37	38	39	40	41	42
43	44	45	46	47	48
49	50	51	52	53	54
55	56	57	58	59	60
61	62	63	64	65	66
67	68	69	70	71	72
73	74	75	76	77	78
79	80	81	82	83	84
85	86	87	88	89	90

Now add up the number of circles in each column:

R _____ I _____ A _____ S _____ E _____ C _____ totals

Which are your three highest scores?

1st _____

2nd _____

3rd _____

Read on for an explanation of your Personality Mosaic.

Interpreting the results

Look over the following description of the six components[1] of the Personality Mosaic and see which one fits you best. Does this description agree with your six scores?

1. Realistic (R)

   THING person who lives in his/her body

   Independent/practical/physically strong/often aggressive/conservative

   Uses hands/eyes to explore things, achieve

   Uses body skillfully, rather than words, thoughts, or feelings

   Requires physical coordination, strength, agility, logic

   Enjoys risk, excitement, being outdoors, concrete problems, money, using tools, large machinery

   Solves problems by doing

2. Investigative *(I)*

   DATA person who lives in his/her mind

   Independent/curious/intellectual/introspective/unconventional

   Uses reading/instruments to explore ideas

   Uses mind/information to achieve, rather than association with people and things

   Requires mental ability, logic, insight

   Enjoys challenge, variety, and complicated, abstract problems

   Solves problems by thinking

3. Artistic (A)

   DATA/THING person who lives in his/her mind, body and feelings

   Creative/sensitive/aesthetic/independent/introspective/expressive/unsocial

   Uses hands/eyes/mind to create new things, writings, ways of doing things

   Requires good eyes, ears, intelligence, perception of color, form, sound, and feelings

   Enjoys beauty, unstructured activity, variety, interesting and unusual sights, sounds, textures, people

   Solves problems by creating

4. Social (S)

   PEOPLE person who lives in his/her feelings

   Concerned leader/sensitive/humanistic/supportive/responsible

   Uses feelings, words, ideas to work with people, rather than physical activity or things

   Requires empathy, tact, perceptiveness, insight, genuineness

   Enjoys closeness, sharing, groups, unstructured activity, being in charge

   Solves problems by feeling

5. Enterprising (*E*)

PEOPLE person who lives in his/her project

Energetic/independent/enthusiastic/confident/dominant/political

Uses mind, words, feelings to deal with people and achieve

Requires sensitivity, insight, assertion, verbal ability, logic

Enjoys organizing, persuading, leading, managing, excitement, variety, status, power, money

Solves problems by risking

6. Conventional (*C*)

DATA person who lives in his/her orderliness

Placid/orderly/careful/accurate

Uses mind, eyes, hands to carry out tasks

Requires logic, care, responsibility

Enjoys order, certainty, security, identifying with power, status

Solves problems by following rules

* * * * * * * * * * * * * * * * *

F O R   T H E   M O S T   P A R T
I do the thing which my
own nature drives
me to do.
—ALBERT EINSTEIN
(from News Summaries 3/19/55)

* * * * * * * * * * * * * * * * *

Here you may wish to go back to the Personality Mosaic and put parentheses around numbers of items that you weren't sure of to see how they change your score. Putting X's on numbers of statements that are *not you* can give you a negative total to show which personality types are least like you.

To get more in touch with yourself, form a group and take turns reading some of the statements for each orientation from the Personality Mosaic. *Be* that kind of person; embellish and dramatize the statements. See how they feel.

The six personality components can be arranged in a hexagon. In this figure the types next to one another are most similar. The words linking them indicate their shared traits or interests. (For example, both artistic and social persons tend to be in tune with their feelings.)

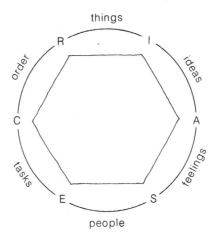

John Holland, *Making Vocational Choices: A Theory of Careers*, © 1973, Personality Types adapted by special permission of John Holland and Prentice-Hall, Inc. C.f. *Self-Directed Search* by John Holland. Copyright © 1970, published by Consulting Psychologists Press, Inc.

Those opposite are most dissimilar. For example, the artistic personality is independent, doesn't mind disorder, and likes to try new things. The conventional person depends more on other people, likes order, and would prefer things to stay the same.

Two people who are strongly opposite in personality can improve their relationship by understanding these differences. A realistic person doesn't deal much with people's feelings, while a social person sees much of life through feelings. That's just the way they are. The introspective "I" person is amazed at the outgoing "E" person.

Fantasize, for a moment, six people sitting around the hexagon. Each person is a strong representative of a personality type. Put a problem in their midst, and each person will solve it in a different way.

Sometimes we have personality conflicts within us. We'd like to be creative, to try something different, but our conventional nature tells us that's a "no-no."

People aren't usually just one type. Most of us are blends of two or three types. Understanding the components of your personality structure can facilitate a good

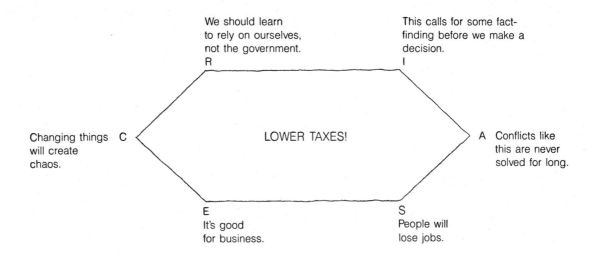

career decision. Understanding the personality structure of others can make for good human relations and easier acceptance of the choices they make. An ideally balanced life contains all six personality elements.

---

the realistic *body needs*	running on the beach planting tomatoes fixing the sink
the investigative *mind needs*	discussing politics reading *War and Peace* planning a trip to Europe
the artistic *aesthetic needs*	enjoying a sunset wearing colors that blend decorating a cake
the social *people needs*	laughing with a friend hugging the baby going to a party
the enterprising *accomplishment needs*	organizing a party saying "Hello" first applying for a job
the conventional *structure needs*	straightening your closet finishing a paper on time stopping at a stop sign

---

Does growth mean allowing all these dimensions to surface and to actualize to the best of your ability? As you grow, will you feel more comfortable in all these areas? A career decision can be in the area of your dominant personality type, a blend of several, or in an area that is quite different from you. You will need extra energy if you veer away from your dominant orientation(s). Be aware of that!

Data, people, things involvement indicator

About 20,000 different occupations have been listed and defined for the United States by the U.S. Department of Labor. The results of this investigation are contained in a monumental work called the *Dictionary of Occupational Titles (DOT)*. It is a gold mine of information—if you know how to dig for the gold. Because of alternate titles for the same job, the 20,000 occupations result in about 40,000 listings. Job titles are listed both alphabetically and by industry. The alphabetical listing gives the code number needed to find a short description of each job among descriptions grouped by occupational area. These clusters of similar jobs make the search easier.[2]

The *DOT* supplement, *Guide for Occupational Exploration*, provides additional help by classifying jobs into 66 job groups. A job group is a cluster of occupations that call for similar worker characteristics.[3]

In the *Dictionary of Occupational Titles*, the 20,000 occupations are classified in three basic categories: data, people, and things. All jobs are involved with data, people, and things on various levels of complexity, but each job can be classified according to which of these three categories is most significant to the worker. Deciding how involved and how responsible you'd like to be in each of these areas gives you a clue to job groups that you would enjoy.

You learned to deal with these three areas at *all levels* early in life. How many times have you planned events, organized people, or fixed things in your lifetime? Some people think of data as complex numbers and computer printouts, but data includes all kinds of ideas and information—the words you speak, read, or listen to, the music you enjoy, the smiles of your friends, and the colors of the sunset. Anything that is not a person or a thing is data.

Now with what you have learned about your personality orientation as background, see how you might enjoy dealing with the *DOT*'s "big three": ideas/ information or data, people, and things. The following three inventories will help you to match some of your traits and interests with groups of jobs that provide your satisfiers. Among 20,000 jobs, there must be one for *you!*

DATA

Words   Numbers   Symbols   Behaviors

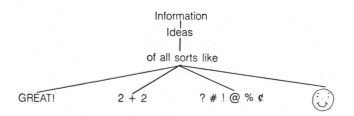

Information
|
Ideas
|
of all sorts like

GREAT!   2 + 2   ? # ! @ % ¢

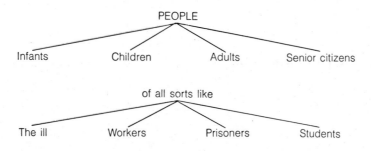

PEOPLE

Infants   Children   Adults   Senior citizens

of all sorts like

The ill   Workers   Prisoners   Students

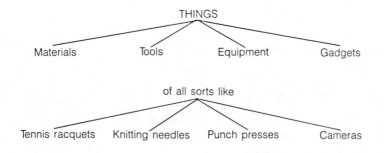

THINGS

Materials   Tools   Equipment   Gadgets

of all sorts like

Tennis racquets   Knitting needles   Punch presses   Cameras

Data, people, things

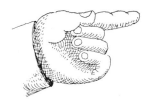

EXERCISES

Working with data

How deeply do you want to get involved with and use data on the job?

Decide which boxes fit you best; then check the space to the right of them.

I prefer doing work that is uncomplicated and easy to learn. I don't mind using information in a simple way if it doesn't require too much mental energy.	☐ Low data

I like keeping track of and working with verbal or numerical information in an orderly way. I prefer having others take responsibility for directing this kind of work.	☐ Medium data

I would enjoy putting ideas and information together to understand complex operations, plan and organize work, and develop new ideas and new ways to do things.	☐ High data

Involvement with people

To what extent do you want to be involved with people as a part of your work?

Decide which boxes fit you best and check the spaces to the right of them.

I prefer involvement with information or things, so I don't mind minimal interaction with people. Being friendly and cooperative with people, giving them information, serving them in some way, is enough people involvement for me.	☐ Low people

I think I would like organizing and motivating people to do a task. I enjoy entertaining people or being a key person in a group.	☐ Medium people

I believe I'd enjoy teaching people, exchanging ideas, negotiating with them to facilitate work activities. I would enjoy helping people deal with complicated personal problems.	☐ High people

Handling things

To what extent would you like to work with things as part of your job?

Check the boxes that fit you best.

I prefer little involvement with things on my job. If I had to work with things, I'd prefer uncomplicated, easy-to-learn procedures.	☐ Low things

I think I would like doing a good job running equipment carefully and correctly but . . . I'd prefer not to have too much responsibility for directing this kind of work.	☐ Medium things

I believe I would enjoy using my hands to work with intricate tools and machines. I'd like to be responsible for a very complex piece of equipment.	☐ High things

Now you know a little about *you* and the big three—*data*, *people*, and *things*. Indicate your rating of H, M, L (high, medium, or low) for each category in the spaces provided below.

Summary:

    D: _____

           P: _____

                  T: _____

Work qualities inventory

The Work Qualities Inventory will help you to identify some of the qualities you'd like your job to have. By rating these qualities, you can zero in on job groups that will be most satisfying to you.

Here are 10 qualities or types of work. These situations or activities are found in many different kinds of jobs. Circle the numbers of work qualities you definitely would like. Put an X on the numbers of those you definitely would not like. If you have never held a job and find it hard to imagine what various jobs are like, think of these qualities in terms of work you've done in school.

1. Work in which you follow a set way of doing things—sometimes over and over again. (Repetition)

2. Work in which you have to be very exact, accurate, and/or make decisions based on set rules or measurements. (Precision)

3. Work in which you have to make decisions based on your best guesses, intuition, or common sense without rules or measurements to go by. (Intuition)

4. Work in which you make, repair, test, process, or otherwise deal with things by using tools, machines, and/or special techniques. (Production)

5. Work in which your duties change often and require you to use different knowledge and skills as they change. (Variety)

6. Work in which you have business contact with people in order to manage, super-vise, negotiate with, teach, or serve them in some way. (Business contact)

7. Work in which you try to persuade/influence people to think or behave in a certain way by interpreting/communicating ideas, facts, or feelings—sometimes very creatively. (Influencing)

8. Work in which you need to get involved in people's personal problems. (Personal contact)

9. Work in which you are recognized as someone important or prestigious or in authority. (Prestige)

10. Work in which you are often under pressure in physically risky, stressful, situations, which sometimes provide adventure and excitement. (Adventure)

Activity analysis

Activity analysis is divided into two parts. To find out what kind of activities are most rewarding to you, you will look for your "Super Six"—the six most satisfying achieve-ments of your life to date. Then you will identify specific skills that you used in order to accomplish the Super Six.

What have you accomplished today? Yesterday? This week? Let your mind flow over all the years of your life, seeing it as a series of achievements, one after the other. These achievements can range from learning to ride a bike, to giving a great party, to renting your first apartment, to making the first team, to making your first million dollars. On a separate sheet of paper, list the achievements that were most satisfying to plan, work for, and accomplish. Then choose six successful activities (see page 26) that you would enjoy repeating. You may want to "sleep on it" and revise the list several times—but don't give up, and don't deceive yourself by saying that you haven't any achievements.

Eight basic skills

When you have narrowed the list down to the Super Six, think about the specific skills that you had to use to accomplish these six activities. Which of the following eight basic skills did you use for each one?

1. I had to concentrate and use my *mind* to figure it out.
2. I had to *read* or *listen* or *talk* to people to get or give information.
3. I used *numbers* to work it out.
4. I had to *visualize* how it would look and *see* small details in its appearance.
5. I had to *check words* or *numbers* for accuracy.
6. I had to choose *colors* that looked good.
7. I had to use my *hands* and *fingers* very carefully.
8. My whole *body*, *eyes*, *hands*, and *feet*, had to work together to do it.

Now list your Super Six below. Then identify the basic skills that you used to accomplish each activity by writing the number of each skill from the list above.

Super Six   Basic skills

1. _____   _____

2. _____   _____

3. _____   _____

4. _____   _____

5. _____   _____

6. _____   _____

Skill satisfaction

These eight skills are *transferable* skills because they can be combined in different ways and used in many different occupations. But perhaps you find yourself using some skills more than others. If so, you are learning which skills give you the most satisfaction. The next step will help you to focus on the skills you enjoy using most. You will be looking for the combination of *mind* and *body* that you use when you are enjoying yourself.

Directions: Check H (high), M (medium), or L (low) for each skill according to the following scale.

H   I would enjoy using this skill with a high level of ability as a major part of my job.

M   I would not mind using this skill with a moderate level of ability as an important part of my job.

L   I would prefer to use this skill only at an easy level or not much at all on my job.

Basic skills	Check here
1. I would like to use *mental energy* on my job because I enjoy thinking planning analyzing evaluating understanding	Intelligence _____ H _____ M _____ L
2. I would like to use *words* on my job because I enjoy reading researching writing listening recording discussing directing instructing communicating motivating	Verbal proficiency _____ H _____ M _____ L

3. I would like to use *numbers* on my job because I enjoy

   figuring

   calculating

   bookkeeping

   budgeting

   analyzing

   Numerical
   proficiency

   _____ H

   _____ M

   _____ L

4. I would like to use my *eyes* for visualization because I enjoy
   visualizing lines on a flat surface or in three dimensions
   comparing lines, figures, spaces, shadings

   Form/space
   awareness

   _____ H

   _____ M

   _____ L

5. I would like to use my *eyes* to check words and numbers
   because I enjoy

   proofreading

   catching errors

   seeing slight differences

   exactness and accuracy

   Clerical
   perception

   _____ H

   _____ M

   _____ L

6. I would like to fill my *eyes* with color because I enjoy

   choosing colors

   using colors

   blending colors

   matching colors

   combining colors

   Color sense

   _____ H

   _____ M

   _____ L

7. I would like using my *fingers* and *hands* in my job because
   I enjoy

   handling

   moving

   assembling

   turning

   operating

   Finger/hand
   agility

   _____ H

   _____ M

   _____ L

8. I would like to use my whole *body* in my job because I enjoy

   carrying

   lifting

   moving

   balancing

   coordinating

   Body
   coordination

   _____ H

   _____ M

   _____ L

Tally sheet

A. List your three highest personality components from the Personality Mosaic on page 63:

     1st _____   2nd _____   3rd _____

B. Indicate your "big three" ratings from the Data, People, Things involvement indicator on page 70:

Data	People	Things
H	H	H
M	M	M
L	L	L

C. Circle the numbers of your "must have" work qualities from the Work Qualities Inventory on page 72, put an X on the numbers of work qualities you prefer to avoid.

1. Repetition
2. Precision
3. Intuition
4. Production
5. Variety
6. Business contact
7. Influencing
8. Personal contact
9. Prestige
10. Adventure

D. Now circle H, M, or L for the eight skill areas from Activities Analysis and Skill Satisfaction, page 74:

1. Mental energy/Intelligence	H	M	L
2. Verbal proficiency	H	M	L
3. Numerical proficiency	H	M	L
4. Space and form awareness	H	M	L
5. Clerical perception	H	M	L
6. Color sense	H	M	L
7. Finger/hand agility	H	M	L
8. Body coordination	H	M	L

The job group chart

You have now discovered your personality orientations, indicated your data/people/ things involvement preference, selected your favorite work qualities, and analyzed your skills. You have begun to find your "satisfiers." The next step is to assemble all of this information about you and match it with job groups from the *Guide for Occupational Exploration.*

A "job group" consists of jobs having similar characteristics. The sixty-six groups are arranged into twelve main areas of interest. The jobs in a given group generally attract people of similar personality types; they call for similar preferences regarding data/ people/ things involvement; they have the same work qualities, and they usually call for the same skills. An example of a job group is "Engineering." There are many kinds of engineering—civil, electrical, mechanical to name a few—but all engineers and engi-neering jobs have many characteristics in common.

These high, medium, and low indicators are generalizations. They are only educated "guesstimates." Some applications are obvious, others are arguable. The indicators are used here not as absolutes, but simply as guides to where your satisfiers are likely to be found.[4]

By following the directions, you will discover which job groups possess your satis-fiers. It is almost as important to *eliminate* groups or even whole interest areas as it is to zero in on job groups of interest. So for example, if involvement with things is definitely not for you, the first page of realistic job groups can probably be crossed out. If you have no interest in the artistic area, cross that off, too. Keep going through the twelve sections of the chart until you have narrowed down your choice. Then choose several job groups of interest to you within these sections. Keep on sifting.

Directions: You are to mark up the chart by circling the indicators listed below. When you have finished, the job groups containing the most circles are most likely to contain your satisfiers, as you see them now.

1. At the far left, circle the numbers of any job groups that are of interest to you.
2. Circle your three highest Personality Types.
3. In the columns marked Data, People, and Things, circle your H, M, or L rating each time it appears in any group, either alone or in a combination, such as HML.
4. Under the column marked Work qualities, circle your "must have" work qualities. Put an X on the work qualities you want to avoid.
5. Under the columns marked Skills, circle your H, M, or L rating for each skill each time it appears in any group.

The Job Group Chart

R - REALISTIC JOB GROUPS

MECHANICAL

	Decimal code	Data D	People P	Things T	Work Qualities	Intelligence 1	Verbal 2	Numerical 3	Form/space 4	Clerical 5	Color 6	Finger/hand 7	Body 8
1. Engineering (dual listed, see p. 80) (Investigative Job Groups)	05.01												
2. Managerial Work–Mechanical: Managing plants or systems where technical work is performed.	05.02	H	ML	L	2,3,4, 5,6,7,9	H	H	HM	HM	M	L	L	L
3. Engineering Technology: Collecting, recording, coordinating technical information.	05.03	H	L	H	2,3,4	HM	M	HM	HM	M	L	HM	L
4. Air and Water Vehicle Operation: Operating planes and ships to carry freight/passengers.	05.04	H	ML	M	2,3,4, 6,9,10	H	HM	HM	HM	M	L	ML	M
5. Craft Technology: Doing highly skilled hand/ machine custom work.	05.05	HM	L	HM	2,3,4, 5	M	L	M	HM	L	L	HM	M
6. Systems Operation: Caring for large, complicated mechanical systems like heating and power.	05.06	HM	L	M	2,4,5, 6	M	M	M	ML	ML	L	ML	L
7. Quality Control: Checking and testing materials and products in nonfactory situations.	05.07	HM	L	HL	1,2, 3,4	M	L	ML	M	L	L	ML	L
8. Land Vehicle Operation: Operating/driving vehicles that haul freight.	05.08	L	L	M	1,2,4	M	L	L	M	L	L	M	M
9. Materials Control: Keeping records of the flow and storage of materials and products.	05.09	M	L	L	1,2, 4,6	M	M	M	L	M	L	ML	L
10. Skilled Hand and Machine Work: Doing moderately skilled hand/machine work	05.10	M	L	HM	1,2,4	L	L	ML	M	L	L	ML	L
11. Equipment Operation: Operating/driving heavy equipment such as in construction, mining.	05.11	L	L	M	1,2,4	M	L	L	M	L	L	M	ML
12. Elemental Work–Mechanical: Doing nonfactory basic manual labor with machines, tools, equipment.	05.12	L	L	ML	1,2,4	L	L	L	ML	L	L	ML	L

INDUSTRIAL (Factory Work)

Item	Code	1	2	3	4	5	6	7	8	9	10	11	12	13
13. Production Technology: Setting up/operating machines to produce goods in specific ways.	06.01	M	ML	H	2,4,6	L	M	M	L	M	L	L	M	L
14. Production Work: Doing hand/machine work to make a product. Also supervising and inspecting.	06.02	ML	ML	M	1,2,4,6	L	ML	ML	L	ML	L	ML	ML	L
15. Quality Control: Testing, weighing, inspecting, measuring products to meet standards.	06.03	ML	L	L	1,2,4	L	L	L	ML	L	ML	L	ML	L
16. Elemental Work–Industrial: Basic manual labor in production requiring little training.	06.04	L	L	L	1,2,4	L	L	L	ML	L	ML	L	ML	L

NATURE

Item	Code	1	2	3	4	5	6	7	8	9	10	11	12	13
17. Managerial Work–Nature: Planning work for farming, fisheries, logging, horticulture.	03.01	H	L	HL	2,3,4,5,6	HM	M	M	M	ML	L	ML	L	L
18. General Supervision–Nature: Supervising on farms, in forests, fisheries, nurseries, parks.	03.02	H	M	HM	2,3,4,5,6,9	M	M	M	M	L	M	L	L	
19. Animal Training and Care: Training, breeding, raising, showing, caring for non-farm animals.	03.03	HML	ML	M	1,2,3,5,7	HM	ML	L	ML	L	ML	ML	ML	ML
20. Elemental Work–Nature: Doing basic physical labor related to farming, fishing, gardening.	03.04	L	L	ML	1,4	L	L	L	ML	L	ML	L	ML	L

PROTECTIVE

Item	Code	1	2	3	4	5	6	7	8	9	10	11	12	13
21. Safety and Law Enforcement: Administration, enforcing laws and regulations.	04.01	H	L	L	3,4,5,6,7,9,10	HM	HM	L	L	M	ML	M	L	L
22. Security Services: Protecting people and property from crime, fire, and other hazards.	04.02	ML	L	ML	1,3,6,10	M	M	L	L	ML	ML	ML	ML	

PHYSICAL PERFORMING

	Decimal code	D Data	P People	T Things	Work Qualities	1 Intelligence	2 Verbal	3 Numerical	4 Form/space	5 Clerical	6 Finger/hand	7 Color	8 Body
23. Sports: Of all sorts; playing, training, coaching and officiating.	12.01	HM	ML	ML	2,3,7, 9,10	M	ML	L	ML	ML	L	H	H
24. Physical Feats: Amusing/entertaining people with special physical skills and strengths.	12.02	M	M	ML	2,3,4, 9,10	M	M	L	HM	L	L	HM	HM

I - INVESTIGATIVE JOB GROUPS

SCIENTIFIC

	Decimal code	D Data	P People	T Things	Work Qualities	1 Intelligence	2 Verbal	3 Numerical	4 Form/space	5 Clerical	6 Finger/hand	7 Color	8 Body
25. Physical Sciences: Research/development in physics, chemistry, geology, computer science.	02.01	H	L	H	2,3,4, 7	H	H	H	HM	M	M	L	L
26. Life Sciences: Studying functions of living things and how they relate to environments.	02.02	H	L	H	2,3,4, 7	H	H	H	HM	M	M	HM	L
27. Medical Sciences: Practicing medicine to prevent, diagnose, cure illnesses of people or animals.	02.03	H	H	H	2,3,5, 7,8,9	H	H	H	H	L	M	HM	L
(1) Engineering: Applying research of science and math to design of new products/systems.	05.01	H	L	H	2,3,4, 5,6,7	H	H	H	HM	L	L	L	L
28. Laboratory Technology: Doing laboratory work to carry out studies of various researchers.	02.04	HM	L	H	2,4	HM	L	HM	HM	ML	M	M	L
29. Mathematics and Statistics: Using numbers and computers to analyze and solve problems.	11.01	H	L	L	2,3,4, 6,7	H	H	H	H	H	L	L	L

A - ARTISTIC JOB GROUPS

ARTISTIC

No. / Job Group	Code	C1	C2	C3	C4	C5	C6	C7	C8	GED	C9	C10	C11
30. Literary Arts: Producing creative pieces from writing to publishing for print, TV, films.	01.01	L	L	L	L	L	L	H	H	3,6,7,9	H	L	L
31. Visual Arts: Doing artistic work, i.e., paintings, designs, photography for personal sale or for media.	01.02	L	HM	H	HM	H	L	L	HM	3,4,6,7	H	H	HM
32. Performing Arts–Drama: Performing in, teaching, stage, radio, TV, film directing productions.	01.03	L	L	L	L	L	L	H	H	3,6,7,9	H	H	H
33. Performing Arts–Music: Playing an instrument, singing, arranging, composing, conducting music.	01.04	H	H	L	HM	HM	HM	HM	HM	3,6,7,9	H	HM	HM
34. Performing Arts–Dance: Performing, teaching, choreographing dance routines.	01.05	H	HM	L	L	HM	L	HL	HM	2,3,6,7,9	H	HM	H
35. Craft Arts: Producing handcrafts, graphics, decorative products.	01.06	L	HM	M	L	HM	L	L	M	2,3,4	M	M	HM
36. Elemental Arts/Amusement: Entertaining and doing novel routines at carnivals, circuses, fairs.	01.07	L	L	L	L	ML	L	M	ML	1,3,6,7	L	M	ML
37. Modeling: Posing for artists; displaying clothing, accessories, other products.	01.08	ML	L	L	L	L	L	L	ML	1,7,9	L	L	L

S - SOCIAL JOB GROUPS

HUMAN SERVICES

No. / Job Group	Code	C1	C2	C3	C4	C5	C6	C7	C8	GED	C9	C10	C11
38. Social Services: Helping people deal with personal, vocational, education, religious concerns.	10.01	L	L	L	L	L	M	H	H	3,5,6,7,8,9	H	HM	L
39. Nursing/Therapy Services: Providing diagnosis and therapy to help people get well.	10.02	ML	ML	ML	ML	M	HM	HM	H	2,3,5,6,7,8	HM	HML	M
40. Child and Adult Care: Assisting with medical and physical care and services.	10.03	L	ML	L	ML	L	L	L	M	1,2,3,5,6,8	M	L	ML

Skills

ACCOMMODATING

	Decimal code	Data (D)	People (P)	Things (T)	Work Qualities	Intelligence 1	Verbal 2	Numerical 3	Form/space 4	Clerical 5	Color 6	Finger/hand 7	Body 8
41. Hospitality Services: Touring, guiding, greeting, serving people to help them feel comfortable.	09.01	HM	ML	L	3,5,6,7,9	M	M	L	L	ML	L	L	L
42. Barber/Beauty Services: Hair and skin care to help people with personal appearances.	09.02	HM	L	H	2,3,4,5,6,7	M	M	L	HM	L	HM	HM	L
43. Passenger Services: Transporting people by vehicle; also instructing and supervising.	09.03	M	L	M	1,2,3,4,6	M	L	ML	M	L	L	M	M
44. Customer Services: Waiting on people in a routine way in a variety of business settings.	09.04	M	L	L	1,4,6	ML	ML	ML	L	ML	L	ML	L
45. Attendant Services: Providing personal services to people at home or when traveling.	09.05	L	L	L	1,6	ML	ML	L	L	L	L	ML	L

S/E - SOCIAL/ENTERPRISING JOB GROUPS

LEADING/INFLUENCING

	Decimal code	Data (D)	People (P)	Things (T)	Work Qualities	Intelligence 1	Verbal 2	Numerical 3	Form/space 4	Clerical 5	Color 6	Finger/hand 7	Body 8
46. Educational/Library Services: Teaching, providing library services.	11.02	HM	HML	L	3,5,6,7,8,9	H	H	M	L	HM	L	L	L
47. Social Research: Studying people of various backgrounds both of the past and present.	11.03	H	L	L	2,3,5,7	H	H	HM	L	HL	L	L	L
48. Law: Counseling, advising, representing people/businesses regarding legal matters.	11.04	H	H	L	2,3,5,6,7,8,9	H	H	HM	L	M	L	L	L
49. Business Administration: Designing procedures, solving problems, supervising people in business.	11.05	H	HML	L	2,3,5,6,7,9	H	H	HM	L	M	L	L	L

No.	Group / Description	Code													
50.	Finance: Setting up financial systems; controlling, analyzing financial records; directing work.	11.06	H	ML	L	2,3,6, 7,9	H	H	H	L	L	HM	L	L	L
51.	Services Administration: Administering programs in an agency such as social, health, educational.	11.07	H	HM	L	3,5,6, 7,8,9	H	H	M	L	L	M	L	L	L
52.	Communications: Writing, editing, translating information for media—print and radio-TV.	11.08	H	L	L	2,3,5, 6,7,9	H	H	M	L	L	M	L	L	L
53.	Promotion: Advertising, fund raising, sales and public relations.	11.09	H	HM	L	3,5,6, 7,9	H	H	HM	L	L	ML	L	L	L
54.	Regulations Enforcement: Checking/enforcing government regulations, company policies, procedures.	11.10	H	L	L	2,3,5, 6,7	HM	HM	M	ML	ML	M	L	L	L
55.	Business Management: Taking responsibility for operation and supervision of a business.	11.11	H	ML	L	2,3,5, 6,9	HM	HM	M	ML	ML	M	L	L	L
56.	Contracts and Claims: Negotiating contracts, investigating claims.	11.12	H	H	L	2,3,5, 6,7,9	H	H	M	L	L	M	L	L	L

E - ENTERPRISING JOB GROUPS

PERSUADING

No.	Group / Description	Code													
57.	Sales Technology: Selling technical equipment or services including insurance. Also clerical work.	08.01	HM	M	L	2,3,6, 7,9	HM	HM	HM	M	L	M	L	L	L
58.	General Sales: Selling goods and services, wholesale/retail to individuals, business or industry.	08.02	M	M	L	2,3,6, 7	M	M	M	L	L	M	L	L	L
59.	Vending: Peddling, promoting items in public settings.	08.03	L	M	L	1,6,7	L	L	ML	L	L	ML	L	ML	L

84

C - CONVENTIONAL JOB GROUPS

BUSINESS DETAIL

	Decimal code	Data D	People P	Things T	Work Qualities	Intelligence 1	Verbal 2	Numerical 3	Form/space 4	Clerical 5	Color 6	Finger/hand 7	Body 8
60. Administrative Detail: Doing secretarial/technical clerical work.	07.01	HM	ML	ML	2,3,5,6,7	HM	HM	M	L	HM	L	L	L
61. Mathematical Detail: Keeping numerical records, doing basic figuring.	07.02	M	L	M	1,2,4,6	M	M	M	L	HM	L	L	L
62. Financial Detail: Keeping track of money-flow to and from the public.	07.03	M	L	ML	1,2,4,6	M	M	M	L	M	L	ML	L
63. Oral Communications: Giving information in person or by communication systems.	07.04	M	L	ML	1,2,4,5,6,7	M	M	ML	L	M	L	ML	L
64. Records Processing: Putting records together and keeping them up-to-date.	07.05	M	L	ML	1,2,6	M	M	ML	L	HM	L	ML	L
65. Clerical Machine Operation: Using various machines to record, process and compute data.	07.06	ML	L	M	1,2,4,6	M	L	L	L	HM	L	HML	L
66. Clerical Handling: Keeping data in order by filing, copying, sorting, delivering.	07.07	L	L	L	1,2,4	ML	ML	L	L	M	L	ML	L

Skills (columns 1–8)

COLLEGE MAJORS The following majors have been arranged by their predominant personality type and by the twelve job group areas; a few have been listed in two places. Check all of those that are of interest to you at this time.

R REALISTIC

Mechanical
___ Aero maintenance/Operations
___ Air conditioning/Refrigeration/ Solar technology
___ Anaplastology
___ Automotive technology
___ Biomedical technology
___ Construction technology
___ Electronics technology
___ See Engineering under I
___ Fabrication technology
___ Food service
___ Industrial administration/ Engineering
___ Industrial engineering and technology
___ Laser technology
___ Machine/Tool technology
___ Manufacturing technology
___ Quality control
___ Radiologic technology
___ Semiconductor management
___ Technological drafting/ Modelbuilding
___ Transportation
___ Welding technology

Industrial
___ No majors

Nature
___ Agriculture
___ Animal health technology
___ Nursery management
___ Park management technology
___ Wildlife management technology

Protective
___ Administration of justice
___ Fire science
___ Safety engineering

Physical performing
___ Physical education/ Kinesiology

I INVESTIGATIVE

Scientific
___ Biological/Life science
___ Agricultural science
___ Animal/Avian science
___ Bacteriology
___ Biology
___ Botany
___ Conservation
___ Enology

I INVESTIGATIVE *continued*

___ Entomology/Pest science
___ Environmental science
___ Food science
___ Forest science
___ Genetics
___ Kinesiology
___ Marine biology
___ Microbiology
___ Nutrition
___ Soil/Water/Wood science
___ Toxicology
___ Zoology
___ Consumer economics/ Science
___ Cybernetics
___ Engineering
___ Aeronautical/Aerospace
___ Agricultural
___ Bio engineering
___ Civil
___ Computer science
___ Electrical/Electronic
___ Environmental
___ Material science
___ Naval architecture
___ Nuclear
___ Science
___ Systems
___ Transportation
___ Linguistics
___ Mathematics/Statistics/ Applied
___ Medical
___ Dentistry
___ Optometry
___ Pharmacy
___ Medicine/Surgery
___ Veterinary medicine
___ Physical sciences
___ Chemistry
___ Geology/Earth science
___ Meteorology
___ Oceanography
___ Physics/Astronomy
___ Social sciences
___ Anthropology
___ Consumer economics
___ Economics
___ Ethnic studies
___ Geography
___ History
___ Psychology
___ Sociology
___ Urban/Rural studies
___ Women's studies

A ARTISTIC

Applied Arts
___ Architecture
___ Commercial art
___ Film/Photography
___ Home economics
___ Fashion design
___ Interior design
___ Industrial design
___ Graphics
___ Journalism
___ Landscape design/ Ornamental horticulture
___ Media specialty
___ Modelbuilding
___ Radio/T.V.
___ Technical illustrating

Fine Arts
___ Art/Art history
___ Dance
___ Drama
___ English
___ Foreign language
___ Humanities
___ Literature
___ Music
___ Philosophy
___ Speech

S SOCIAL

Human services
___ Community health worker
___ Counseling
___ Dental assistant/hygiene
___ Dietician
___ Health science
___ Inhalation therapy
___ Nursing RN, LVN, assistant
___ Occupational therapy
___ Pediatric assistant
___ Physical therapy/also assistant
___ Primary care associate
___ Psychiatric technician
___ Psychology-clinical
___ Public health
___ Social service
___ Speech pathology and audiology

Accommodating
___ Cosmetology
___ Food service
___ Travel careers

S/E SOCIAL/ENTERPRISING

Leading-influencing
___ Advertising
___ Business administration
___ Convalescent hospital administration
___ Education
___ Health care management
___ Insurance
___ Labor studies
___ Law
___ Library science
___ Management/Supervision
___ Manpower administration
___ Office administration
___ Public relations
___ Recreation
___ See Social science under I
___ Volunteer administration

E ENTERPRISING

Persuading
___ Business administration
___ Fashion/Retail merchandising
___ International trade
___ Law
___ Marketing/Sales
___ Political science
___ Purchasing
___ Real estate
___ Speech

C CONVENTIONAL

Business Detail
___ Accounting
___ Attorney assistant
___ Banking
___ Court reporting
___ Data processing
___ Insurance
___ Secretarial
___ Administrative
___ Clerical
___ Medical assistant/Records
___ Legal
___ Unit clerk
___ Word processing

The career target

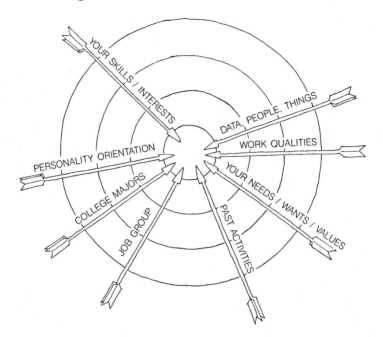

By now you should have your chart well marked. Notice in which of the twelve interest areas your circles tend to cluster. Notice which of the 66 job groups have your most important satisfiers. Some of the circled satisfiers may carry more weight for you than others. Some of them may be used in settings you would not like. You have hit the bullseye whenever your likes and skills fit together neatly—on target—into a job group.

When you feel you've zeroed in on some job groups that have traits you prefer, you might like more information. You can look up the job groups in the 1979 *DOT*, *Guide for Occupational Exploration*, in career centers, library reference rooms, and state employment offices. Use the decimal code number from the job chart for easy reference.

List your top three job groups here.

1. _____

2. _____

3. _____

At this point you might be feeling a little scared/anxious/uncertain/confused. These are all normal feelings for anyone on the verge of a *great discovery!* Keep going! Don't be overwhelmed if you find that several jobs look good to you. Some people are comfortable in a number of areas. Sometimes a person needs more experience with work before making a decision. Give yourself more time if you need it. Don't decide to decide without seeing clearly.

There are still other things you can look at to help your decision along. Finding out about projected job market trends for your areas of interest can be helpful here. But one of the best ways to decide is to get some "inside information," through work experience, group tours of work places, or interviewing people who work in your area of interest. The rest of this manual will give you some help with these concerns.

Making a good career decision is a growth process, and growth takes patience. You can't make a flower grow by pulling on it.

Five ▸ The job market:

PAST ⟶

NOW ↓

⟵ FUTURE

Trends and predictions

There is a small factor about choosing a career that you may wish to glance at: the job market, or *Who needs you out there?* The truth is, there is no really accurate way to tell. There are all sorts of charts and statistics that try to tell you how many plumbers will be needed in Chicago in 1988. But how does that relate to *you* if you'll be ready to go plumbing in 1986? And even if people need plumbers, will they need *you*? And how many other plumbers will be in the line with you? And . . .???

So rather than simply look at numbers, let's consider the job market in the much larger context of trends in society. Don't avoid the statistics. Use all the help you can get in finding out the projected need for your particular occupation. But it may help to see this projection against a backdrop of ruminations about change in society.

A profile of the future

Alvin Toeffler coined the term "Future Shock" to describe the effect of increasingly rapid changes in our society on our poor, slow-to-catch-up psyches. Joseph Luft constructed (from Toeffler's writings) a profile of some of the factors reflecting transience and disorientation brought on by the premature arrival of the future with its radical impact on man and society.*

1. *Population*—The time required to double the world's population dropped from 1 billion years to 1,000 years, to 200 years, to 80 years. At the present

*From Joseph Luft, *Group Processes: An Introduction to Group Dynamics* (Palo Alto, Calif.: Mayfield, 1970.) Reprinted with permission

accelerated rate of population growth, the earth's population will double in 35 years.

2. *Production*—The gross national product of goods and services in the 21 advanced nations of the world is doubling every decade-and-a-half.

3. *Scientists*—Between 85 percent and 95 percent of all scientists who ever lived were alive in 1970.

4. *Energy*—Approximately half the energy consumed in the last 2,000 years has been consumed in the last 100 years.

5. *Speed*—The top speeds of transportation never exceeded 20 m.p.h. until the mid-nineteenth century. Rockets now travel at over 20,000 m.p.h. and commuter speed exceeds the speed of sound.

6. *Innovation*—The innovative cycle between a new idea and its application has shortened from as much as a millenium to a few years. Combinations of inventions, including those using computers, have drastically speeded up new inventions.

7. *Moving*—Approximately 36 million people move from one place to another each year in the United States.

8. *Books*—In four-and-a-half centuries the publication of new books has increased from 1,000 a year to 1,000 a day.

9. *Scientific literature*—The number of journals and articles appears to be doubling every 15 years, with current output of some 20 million pages per year.

10. *Information*—The number of words and ideas taken in daily by the average adult from newspapers, magazines, radios, and television has risen sharply, and new technologies to increase the speed of information flow proliferate at a rapid rate.

Trends develop, and before we can digest their implications, a countertrend is in progress. In the 1950's cities encouraged growth, and the postwar influx of workers caused city populations to zoom. City planning became imperative as attendant problems of congestion, pollution, and just plain confusion increased. Our attention became firmly riveted on these concerns, which we've barely begun to solve. Behold, in the 1970's we glance up to find the population of cities is diminishing, while small towns and rural areas are growing.

We've seen conflicting trends, from college for upward mobility to college for unemployment, baby-booms to Zero Population Growth, planning for the huge and a longing for the small. We've seen the sexual revolution, the women's movement, radical changes in lifestyle, increasing divorce, religious movements away from established religion—and toward older, more established religion. All of these things challenge our deepest values and make us feel like strangers in a strange land. We live in a "new world" and it seems to get "newer" every day. Each alteration causes far-reaching changes in many areas of the job market. And predicting this market becomes increasingly difficult as these movements occur more rapidly.

We seem to be developing gradually into a transactional society: one in which the predominant form of work consists of abstract transactions between people. As described by Jean Gottman, Professor of Geography at Oxford University and author of *Megalopolis*, this change is the result of an increase in technological advances and a decrease in the need for physical labor.[1] It is awesome to visit automated warehouses, power plants, and other work sites where silent computers initiate, direct, and terminate complex and heavy work. And yet, watch for the countertrend. Increasing costs of automation and high unemployment cause some employers to delay these investments. Some are hiring low-cost human labor instead.

Productivity is an important factor in inflation management. But productivity is becoming less relevant as production occupations decrease and service and knowledge occupations increase. So inflation soars as we involve ourselves more and more in data.

Engineers, planners, designers spend their days poring over thick computer printouts, often not seeing any concrete results of their work except a model or a picture. This kind of work involves a high level of sophistication, an unusual ability to communicate, and the ability to understand an endless stream of copier and computer produce that is in its way perhaps more demanding than work required of the laborer of old.

We may someday become so automated and sophisticated that we will do much of our work at home by computer.

Population studies are also essential in describing the job market. They tell us how many people will be competing for jobs and what goods and services will be required.

For example, the baby boom of the fifties (1946–61) added 60 million people to the population, compared to the 40 million born in the previous fifteen years. This group, born into unprecedented affluence, has affected such diverse areas of life as education, the crime rate, unemployment, and entertainment.

The rebellious teenagers of the sixties are now the young adult group of the seventies and eighties: many of them conservative, mortgage-holding new parents buying furniture and other expensive items. They are now competing for jobs, and each new job requires a capital outlay of some sort: a place to work, equipment, staff, capital reserves, all of which diminish in time of inflation.

In the year 2020 they will constitute a uniquely large group of senior citizens. According to Terry Kirkpatrick of Associated Press, "They will be remembered as the generation that stood in line."

Another important result of population and technology developments is that full employment in the old sense may never be seen again. What are some of the effects of unemployment? Usually thought to be disastrous and humiliating, unemployment can often produce a feeling of euphoria at not having to meet the daily grind. Men especially have had little hope of reprieve from a life-long sentence to the forty-hour week. A layoff can be a liberating experience, provided one doesn't grow too hungry. A layoff is a good time to reevaluate a career and make changes. Many people have changed from the corporate complex to small business ownership. From designing gas guzzlers to designing sandwiches in their own delis, from making hardware to making beds in their guest cottages by the sea, many laid-off persons are "so glad they made the change" as a result of unemployment.

People have created "new ways to work," such as job sharing, alternating male/female roles in child and house care, and "flextime." When people cut down their work involvement, they free jobs for others. In California, *New Ways to Work* in Palo Alto is helping people present themselves to employers in such unique ways. The sponsors feel that "there are just not enough jobs to go around unless the work is shared." Job sharing can be a good way for two people to find part-time employment, especially when child care or other commitments preclude full-time work. But many employers need to be convinced of its value. At present, its effect on the job market is negligible.

Tomorrow's jobs

Nobody can predict the future with absolute certainty, and therefore nobody can say exactly which jobs will be numerous and which will die out in the next few years. But we can look at the way people are living and begin to see patterns taking shape for the future. Experts can make tentative predictions about tomorrow's jobs.

P. J. Michelozzi has compiled a list of ten trends and predictions from the *Occupational Outlook Handbook*[2] and *Manpower Report of the President.*[3] Below are ten factors that will shape the future and some of the effects that these social trends will have on the job market:

Limited population growth: The average family has decreased from three children to two children, and the trend is expected to continue.

- Less need for pediatricians and maternity wards
- In twenty to thirty years, more old people, fewer young workers
- Less need for large homes—possibly less need for new homes—hence less work in construction. Yet there are many potential home owners among the large population in their twenties. Will inflated housing costs prevent home ownership?
- Less need for goods and services for children (toys, medicines, baby food, and so on)
- Less demand for teachers and new schools

Women's movement: Women feel freer to leave the homemaking role, go to work, and compete with men.

- More child-care centers

- More convenience foods, household appliances, synthetic fabrics (easy wash and dry)
- Women compete with men for more white collar jobs
- More professional house cleaning services

More elderly people: Better medical care enables more people to live longer.

- More goods and services for older people
- More health services for older people—nursing homes, retirement housing, more doctors specializing in health care for the elderly
- Increased need for adult education, enrichment courses, senior citizen programs
- Recreational programs, jobs for travel agencies and the transportation industry, social programs, senior centers

Higher family incomes: The increase is due to higher salaries, labor negotiations, and more working wives.

- More recreational demands—campers, motor homes, sports equipment, boats—creating jobs for people who make them, sell them, service them
- More people using credit, borrowing money—enhancing employment in agencies, loan companies, banks
- More travel calling for more travel agents, aviation industry workers, such as flight attendants, aircraft mechanics, air traffic controllers, and so on. (Air travel will keep on growing; rail travel will decrease.)
- Demand for better services increasing consumer advocate functions
- More buying of factory-made goods, hence manufacturing occupations in selected areas where automation does not replace workers
- Better nutrition increasing employment in health foods industry
- More and more varied insurance protection increasing employment in insurance industry

Ecology crisis: Pollution and energy shortages have made people aware of new tasks and changes that are needed to protect the environment.

- More urban planners, increases in urban renewal, and the necessary construction work involved
- More mass transit planning/construction/operation
- Newly created ecology-oriented occupations in energy conservation, and new sources of energy; need for special teachers to retrain people for these new jobs
- Better sanitation services requiring garbage manipulators, workers in water control and purification, pollution clean-up, recycling

Automation: Machines are doing more and more work previously done by hand.

- Fewer production/manufacturing jobs (blue collar jobs)
- More skills needed
- Job re-training
- More computer use, hence good opportunities in computer industry

Reprinted with permission
Washington Star Syndicate, Inc.

Super business: Small businesses are being eliminated by large chains that can sell products and services more cheaply.

- Fewer small businesses (such as corner grocery stores)
- More jobs in supermarkets and department stores, including jobs for sales people, store managers, business managers, cashiers, clerks, accountants, data processors, computer programmers
- More vending machines and self-service—hence need for replenishers and repairmen
- More jobs for people trained in business—secretaries, accountants, book-keepers, office workers
- Continued increase in transportation occupations

Urbanization: Most of the U.S. population is clustered in or around cities—but the trend is beginning to reverse.

- Demand for more city, county, and state services—parks, roads, police, firemen, probation officers, secretaries, sanitation, welfare services, and so on
- More mass transit systems and transit industry occupations

Higher mobility: People move more often—job transfers, job changes, new starts, better opportunities, early retirement—but a new trend says "Stay put!"

- Continued high level of real estate transactions
- Continued availability of jobs in transportation and moving industries

What else? Unexpected trends develop from time to time.

- Effective taxpayers' revolts affecting government jobs, which in turn will ripple into other areas
- Inflation consuming increased income
- Countertrends to all of the above, such as "voluntary simplicity" involving people's need to simplify their lives and use fewer resources

Good job hunting

The *Occupational Outlook Handbook*, published by the U.S. Department of Labor, is one of the best beginning references for a job search. Generally available in any library, the handbook provides a good overview of 800 of the most popular careers in the United States. It outlines the nature of the work, average earnings, training requirements, and places to write for further information, along with the projected employment outlook.

A study by Dr. Leonard Lecht for the U.S. Office of Education gives the following general predictions up to 1985:

Good job hunting
- in technical, managerial, and health occupations
- as replacements for older workers in vacancies resulting from retirement and attrition
- for those with marketable skills obtained in a vocational program in high school, community college, or a technical institute

Declining jobs
- for agricultural workers
- for blue-collar workers
- for the unskilled

Between 1976 and 1985 (according to the Bureau of Labor Statistics) 10.4 million college graduates will enter the labor force, and 2.7 million will be unable to find jobs that fit their abilities or expectations. So a degree will decline in value but will still have greater earning power than a high school diploma. There is no doubt that a college education enhances skills at many levels.[4]

HERMAN *by Unger*

If I have to keep going to school, all the best jobs are going to be snapped up.

Copyright 1977
Universal Press Syndicate

Personality types in the job market

Understanding your own personality is vital to your career search. You should know, for example, whether you are happier working indoors quietly seated at a desk or outdoors actively moving around. Observe yourself throughout the day to find out where you feel most comfortable.

Remember the six personality types: realistic, investigative, artistic, social, enterprising, and conventional.* Specific jobs can be related to each type. By observing yourself, perhaps you will identify with one of these six types and find a suitable career on one of the lists below. The lists are jobs predicted by the Department of Labor (DOL) to be among the fastest growing jobs until 1985.[5]

*John Holland, *Making Vocational Choices: A Theory of Careers*, © 1973. Personality Types adapted by special permission of John Holland and Prentice-Hall, Inc.

Realistic type

Jobs for the Realistic Type are generally involved with things and with data as required instead of people. Usually these jobs use some body skills. Examples range from various trades and crafts to professional sports. Careers in sports, of course, are extremely competitive and limited to the most talented. But the employment outlook is good to excellent for many jobs in the realistic category.

If you feel you are strongly thing-oriented, you might consider indoor or outdoor jobs in industry or with the public utility companies. You may want special vocational training, although on-the-job training is sometimes available. In the building trades, you may be required to join a union as an apprentice. Cutbacks in government spending have limited the number of outdoor jobs available to people who like to work with nature.

Volunteering is a way to get training and work experience in some of these jobs. Sometimes realistic persons build unique and creative careers by cooking, tailoring, or cabinetmaking at home. If you see yourself as the Realistic Type, consider the following fast-growing jobs:

Air conditioning/Refrigeration mechanics
Airplane mechanics
Air traffic controllers
Assemblers
Boat motor mechanics
Boilermakers
Building custodians
Computer science technicians
Concrete finishers
Construction inspectors
Construction machinery operators
Cooks and chefs
Dental lab technicians
Diesel mechanics
Dispensing opticians
Drafters
Drywall installers
Electricians
Elevator constructors
Engineering technicians
Food counter workers
Forestry technicians
Glaziers
Health regulatory inspectors
Industrial machinery repairers
Insulation workers
Ironworkers
Lithographers
Manufacturing inspectors
Motorcycle mechanics
Occupational safety workers
Ophthalmic lab technicians
Pest controllers
Photo lab technicians
Plumbers/Pipefitters
Range managers
Roofers
Security guards
Security system installers
Surveyors
Truck/Bus mechanics
TV servicers
Waste water plant workers
Welders

Investigative type

Jobs for the Investigative Type are high-data jobs and, except for the medical area, have little people involvement. They usually use above average intelligence and verbal and/or mathematical skills. Many require a college education, at least at the A.A. level. Most jobs in this area require thinking about things, rather than working with things.

Many of the jobs in the scientific area are not directly "productive" because they deal with "pure research." Since there are no products or direct services to be sold for profit, funding tends to be less abundant than in the Realistic category. Engineers and medical researchers are exceptions. They bridge the gap by doing research that applies directly to practical problems. Hence more jobs are available in these categories.

Generally there are good job possibilities in all Investigative Type areas except pure research. The *DOL* lists these jobs among the fastest growing to 1985:

Actuaries	Medical lab workers
Biochemists	Programmers
Doctors	Statisticians
Economists	Systems analysts
Engineers	Urban planners
Geologists	Veterinarians
Geophysicists	X-ray technicians

Artistic type

Most jobs and job groups for the Artistic Type use special talent along with training. They are usually high-data and/or thing jobs, with no deep involvement with people. Artistic persons enjoy creating new things but often dislike the mass producing and marketing aspects of making a living. Business pressure often militates against creativity. Many highly creative people also find it hard to work in structured settings doing work for others, such as architecture, advertising, and various other design jobs.

Artistic jobs tend to be highly competitive, so the Artistic Type should plan solid alternatives. Only two artistic-personality careers are listed by the *DOL* as fast growing to 1985: floral designers and landscape architects.

Social type

Social-personality careers deal primarily with people, although the more complex jobs involve data also. Workers should be good with people, concerned with people's problems, or at least comfortable providing services to people.

Many of the jobs in the social services area are government funded. Because of tax cutbacks, jobs are scarce in some states at present, though many people do well in private practice. Some government jobs in human services defeat the purpose of helping people: Workers in some settings are drained by large numbers of clients with serious and chronic problems. With little support, few resources, and yards of red tape, the worker needs strong motivation to succeed.

Health care is a growing field, but in many localities entrance into training programs is limited. People with social concerns find that their special talents can be used in a variety of ways, however, because all areas of work employ people and need solutions to people problems.

The *DOL* cites these job titles as fastest growing to 1985:

Dental assistants	Operating room technicians
Dental hygienists	Physical therapists/Assistants
EKG/EEG technicians	Recreation workers
Emergency medical technicians	Respiratory therapists
Nurses	Social workers/Aides
Nursing aides	Speech therapists
Occupational therapists/Assistants	

Enterprising type

The Enterprising Type is usually a person of energy, courage, and confidence who loves the "game" of selling, persuading, risking, and motivating. Generally, men have been socialized to strive for success with courage and confidence—whether they like it or not—but women have been socialized for a commitment to people instead of accomplishment. The ideal personality for these jobs achieves a balance between striving to accomplish and being sensitive to people.

Many jobs in this category require both "drive" and "good people skills"—the Social and Enterprising Types combined. Those who have or can develop both traits will usually be successful. These are all high-data jobs requiring intelligence and good verbal skills. There are always good job possibilities for those with talent, and the *DOL* lists these specific jobs as fastest growing to 1985:

Auto salespersons	Personnel and labor relations workers
Bank officers	Public relations workers
Health service administrators	Purchasing agents
Marketing researchers	Travel agents
Personnel administrators	

Conventional type

Conventional-personality careers require steadiness, orderliness, and accuracy in dealing with data. They require tolerance for paperwork, and at times involve business contact with people. Workers who favor this orientation are usually content where they are and don't wish to move up. Experience may build their confidence and give them the courage to advance, but generally they do well in a supportive role.

There are many careers that demand the steadiness and order of the conventional personality. The *DOL* lists these job titles as the fastest growing to 1985:

Bank clerks	Medical record administrators
Business machine operators	Medical record technicians
Cashiers	Optometric assistants
Collection workers	Receptionists
Computer operators	Typists
Medical assistants	

Many predictions of trends related to the job market are based on dated information; yet, surprisingly, job predictors are remarkably accurate. Some things to remember:

- Labor market statistics are based on random samples—not on 100 percent of the population—but you can use them to learn about trends.
- Even though a job title is listed as "fast growing," you may not be able to find a job in this field. Check the degree of competition and the number of actual jobs available.
- Local geographic trends may be more important than national trends. Talk to people, consult the local state employment office, and know the dynamics of your area.
- Many skills are transferable. If the occupation of your choice is impacted, consider other careers that utilize the same skills and offer similar satisfiers.
- No one can guarantee you a job after you have invested many years and dollars training for it. How much are you willing to risk? How motivated are you? Have you looked for ways to use your training in alternate choices?

Brainstorming alternatives

No problem, you think. You have decided on *the* career. Ever since high school when Mr. Yesteryears turned you on to the Peloponnesian Wars, you have wanted to be a history teacher, just like him. You could hear your students sighing "Wow,

I never knew history could be so great!" Slowly into your fantasy seeps the news that there are hundreds of unemployed history teachers. The bubble bursts.

But wait. All is not lost. Have you considered alternatives? Think over the various elements that make up a career. For example, where in the world are you willing to go to teach history? Germany? Australia? Does Alaska need you? The Peace Corps?

What do you *need* from your career? Is it history or the audience or both, for example? What can you do with a history background that will give you the *audience* you would enjoy? Consider:

- Developing a unique lecture series on a topic of current interest such as the architectural history of Victorian homes in Dubuque, to present to community groups
- Tutoring
- Learning to be a docent
- Working as a tour guide
- Working as an historian for the State Parks and Recreation Department
- Getting involved in politics
- What else?

If you can get along with "just history" without teaching, consider:

- Developing a tour series on tape or by map—for example, a walking historical tour of Atlanta
- Writing news articles about historical subjects, such as the Indians of the upper Michigan Peninsula
- Working in a library or book store and specializing "on the side" in historical books of all sorts
- Planning historical tours
- What else?

Perhaps, after thinking it over again, you would enjoy the idea of just teaching—having people listen to you and learn from you. Consider:

- Other teaching areas that still have openings (check school districts for local trends)
- Volunteering in schools, recreation centers, senior citizen centers, working as a teacher aide
- Teaching small classes at home or to outside community groups, such as the P.T.A., Girl/Boy Scouts
- Teaching cooking, macrame, vegetable gardening, or house plant care
- What else?

With a little work some of those activities can be parlayed into a lucrative business, but others cannot. A job must fulfill the needs of other people to such an extent that they will part with money to fulfill those needs. For people who would like to teach and earn a more secure living, an often overlooked area is industry. Larger industries, especially, have training programs/orientations for new employees and in-service training for continuing employees. Someone must be "teacher" in these industrial settings.

✳ ✳ ✳ ✳ ✳ ✳ ✳ ✳ ✳ ✳ ✳ ✳ ✳ ✳

T H E   F I R S T   T H I N G
to do in life is to do
with purpose
what one proposes to do.
—PABLO CASALS

✳ ✳ ✳ ✳ ✳ ✳ ✳ ✳ ✳ ✳ ✳ ✳ ✳ ✳

Working in marketing and sales, public relations, or personnel, including such areas as job development or affirmative action, can involve you in many situations similar to teaching: giving site tours, helping people find employment, and working with other people problems that arise.

Go back to the DOT Data, People, Things Indicator and the job groups and consider the factors that are important to you. Consider related jobs again and *brainstorm*, *brainstorm*, with friends, relatives, neighbors, acquaintances, strangers, anyone who will give you five minutes of their time and a dip into their experience pool. For just about any career that you can choose, there are alternatives that give you most of what you would enjoy from a job.

If you still want more than anything to be a history teacher, if your motivation for that one career is unusually high, don't be afraid to face the competition. Develop some unique skills by getting involved in some of the above alternatives to get super-good at history and teaching. Keep open to alternatives, but keep to your chosen goals.

A few more ideas to get you going:

■   Volunteer experience can be extremely valuable in skill development. It wouldn't do to stay in the back room and lick stamps, however, unless licking stamps is your goal. Pinpoint the skills you would like to develop. When you volunteer, ask for experience doing these things: public relations, fund raising, supervising people, organizing materials, activities, and such. Be specific.

- Be sure to review your volunteer experience for skills you've already developed: writing good letters, directing membership drives, and so on. Be very specific about your accomplishments.

- Don't overlook entry-level or support-service job skills, such as typing and cashiering, to gain access to businesses of interest to you. You can often then work into jobs closer to your interest field in places from art galleries to auto shops by beginning "at the bottom."

- Take skill courses that can help you gain access to jobs. For example, most banks train tellers on the job but might be willing to hire someone with training in accounting or office procedures.

- Use your main career interest as a hobby while you work at something else to support yourself. Walter Chandoha pursued a business degree while maintaining an interest in photographing cats. He has been a professional animal photographer for more than ten years now and is doing better than he ever dreamed.[6] Maybe his business background has been a help!

- Investigate training programs in various industries and government agencies.

- Consider earning extra money, perhaps at home, through cooking, hobbies, and crafts or teaching them. For example, think about:

Catering, special food services	Aprons
Cake decorating	Embroidering shirts, jeans
Picture framing	Sewing alterations
Dried flower arrangements	Knitting
Sculpture	Crocheting
Shadow boxes	Painting
Macrame	Furniture re-finishing
Weaving	Stained glass
Hand puppets, dolls, and doll clothes	Decoupage
	Pet care

Also consider teaching recreation skills:

Dancing	Riding
Yoga	Swimming
Music	Bridge
Exercise	Tennis
Skiing	Golf
Massage	

Advertise your skills and classes through friends, supermarket bulletin boards, local community groups. Donate samples and demonstrations.

Other creative careers:

House sitting
Shop sitting
Pet sitting
Providing travel/transportation companions to match
Creative child sitting where you might provide instruction in a craft or some
    hobby
Shopping for others—for example, the elderly at Christmas
Transportation for the elderly, handicapped
Photography at special events or with children
House calls on sick plants
Giant cookies
Tasty diet candy
Exercise groups for the elderly
Masquerading servants at parties
Do-it-yourself garage managers/instructors in auto service

Careers to do at home:

Typing, perhaps in a medical, technical, scientific, or legal specialty
Translating
Telephone wake-up service
Singing messages
Designing:
    Stationery
    Business cards
    Party favors
    What else?
Recycling:
    Clothes
    Furniture
    Household appliances
Income tax service
Tool/gadget repair and maintenance

Consider direct selling for companies such as Avon, Tupperware, Cutco, and
others of good reputation. Write for member list and consumer education. Enclose
a long, stamped, self-addressed envelope to: Direct Selling Association, Dept. A,
1730 M St. N.W., Washington, D.C. 20046. Find *Direct Mail and Mail Order
Handbook* by Richard S. Hodgson (Dartnell) and *Successful Direct Marketing
Methods* by Bob Stone (Crain Communications) in the business reference section
of your public library. Get *Mail Order Enterprises* for $1 at any Bank of America
branch or from *Small Business Reporter*, Bank of America, Dept. 3120, P.O. Box
37000, San Francisco, CA 94137. Request free *Tips on Work-at-Home Schemes*

and *Tips on Mail Order Profit Mirages* from the Council of Better Business Bureaus,
Inc., 1150 17th St. N.W., Washington, D.C. 20046. Write to the Small Business Administration, Washington, D.C., 20416, for *Small Business Bibliography No. 3 (Selling by Mail Order)* or pick up a copy in any SBA field office.[7]

Consider temporary employment: One of the local agencies can provide a way to survey businesses, make contacts, make money on your own schedule.

Keep your options open. The narrower your "satisfaction band," the less likely you are to achieve satisfaction. In other words, the more options the better.

When you have done everything you can but end up with a job you don't care for, you still have some choices:

- Watch for opportunities within the business
- Re-train at night or get further training
- Create your own career within a career—some people have found exciting things to do in apparently the dullest and most stifling of situations.

Some people create so much joy within themselves that they are happy anywhere. Perhaps that, after all, is the key to success.

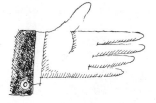

EXERCISES: THE JOB MARKET

1. To what extent are you going to let job market statistics determine your career choice?

_____

_____

_____

2. What effect does "Future Shock" have on you?

_____

_____

_____

3. Which of the ten trends could limit your choice of careers?

_____

_____

_____

4. What trends or countertrends could help your career choice?

_____

_____

_____

5. Do your career choices center around "transactions" as defined by Jean Gottman? How?

_____

_____

_____

6. How could you set up a job-sharing situation in the career of your choice? How would you present this idea to a prospective employer?

_____

_____

_____

7. Of what use is a college degree?

_____

_____

_____

8. What are the general job prospects for your personality orientation?

_____

_____

_____

9. What does the *Occupational Outlook Handbook* say about your career choice?

_____

_____

_____

10. Discuss career alternatives for your job choice and alternate work styles for your career.

_____

_____

_____

Six  Breaking and entering:

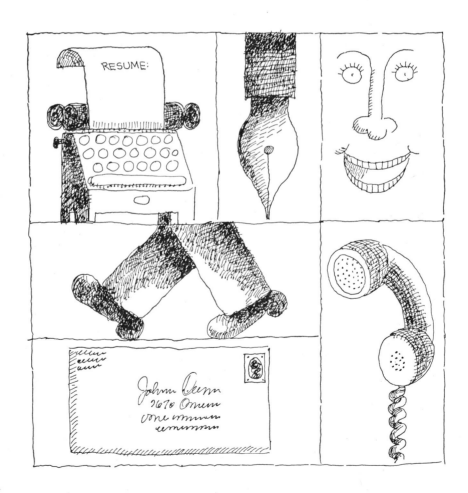

Tools for
the job hunt

Unless you are an experienced and sophisticated job seeker with a broad knowledge of jobs, it is important to do some homework before you start job hunting.

First, be sure that you've read as much as possible about your interest areas. Use career center and other libraries until you feel knowledgeable.

Second, begin to gather information about companies. Start with the Yellow Pages of your phone book. Get acquainted with your local librarian and ask for help with the business reference section. A great deal of data is available about companies, especially the larger ones. Many periodicals can be helpful. For example, *Money* published an article in November 1976 titled, "Ten Terrific Companies to Work For."[1] Articles like this would be worth reading just to become more aware of things to look for. The Chamber of Commerce is another resource. Some state employment offices also may be stocked with material about companies. Some companies have public relations departments that send information if you write or call.

Third, after you've researched your field and found companies where you could do work you would enjoy, begin your career observation. It is important to *see* real live people doing a job that you think might suit you. There are a number of ways to do this.

One way is to get a job at a place that employs people in your chosen career. It doesn't have to be a full-time, permanent, paid position. If the health fields interest you, for example, volunteer at a hospital as a "pink lady" or candy striper. Or sign up at a temporary employment agency—one with a good reputation—and research many people at many companies while you earn some money. Get acquainted with people in the cafeteria, for example. Try your school or state employment placement office for positions at different workplaces. Some com-

109

panies have tours that you can take. In some cases you can spend a whole day observing someone doing a job you might like.

Become *career aware*. Talk to friends, relatives, and everyone you meet about what they do. Then ask them if they can introduce you to someone in your career field of interest. Very often resources are right in front of us, but we don't see them. Read the newspaper, especially the financial pages. Don't be afraid to call or write to people who seem interesting. Ask them to tell you more about what they do, or congratulate them on some accomplishment or promotion. Let them know if you are sincerely interested in some aspect of the company. People appreciate positive feedback.

Remember, when you talk with people in your career field of interest, you are gathering all their biases. Each person likes and dislikes certain things about the job. Each one will give you a different view. Keep your antennae out to receive the emotional content of their messages. And then weigh all these messages against *your* good feeling and reasoned judgment.

By the time you are ready for an interview, you will understand the job and its problems. You will know the latest techniques being used. You will know people in the field who may recommend or even hire you. Remember: 80 percent of all jobs are acquired by word of mouth, and now you will be in the hiring network!

The job may require special education and training. Why not find out all you can before spending time and money on training for a job you may not like? You can clarify misconceptions about the preparation you need in order to be hired.

If you feel timid about approaching a stranger, begin by interviewing someone in your family, then a friend or neighbor, about his or her job. Ask people you know for names of willing interviewees. It's amazing how you can usually find someone who knows someone who knows someone. . . .

If you feel uncertain about going to an interview alone, ask a friend to introduce you, or ask someone with a mutual interest to go along. Invite the people to be interviewed out for coffee or lunch after you visit their workplaces—always ahead of time by appointment—at their convenience. If you want things to go smoothly, do not drop in on a busy person unexpectedly.

Use the information interview sparingly, not casually. Wait until you have done all your homework carefully and have some idea of your direction. Most people are sincerely interested in helping information seekers but sometimes they cannot afford the time. Don't feel discouraged if you are refused an interview.

Also seek someone close to the level at which you are applying. Don't ask to see the president of a company if you are searching out information about safety engineering. Rather, find a person who is a safety engineer, or industrial technologist, or technical supervisor.

There are other ways to meet people in your field of interest. Many professional groups welcome students at their meetings and have special rates for student/lay participation. The Society of Women Engineers is one of these. The Chamber of Commerce and various community clubs have luncheons with speakers. In social settings like these, it's possible to make contacts easily and explore possibilities for on-site visits. By attending workshops or classes in your career area of interest, you may find that speakers and participants can share information with you both formally and informally. Much of your success will come from keeping your eyes and ears open. Become *career aware*. Begin to wonder what just about everyone you meet is *doing*. Almost every media news item is about people's doings. Which ones attract you? How can you find out more? Keep looking, listening, and asking questions. It's your best source of information.

Keep practicing and enlarging your "bravery scope." Be prepared for some job offers as your confidence grows. By the time you go to a real interview, it will be duck soup instead of sitting duck.

Guidelines for research

At first you'll need some guidelines to prepare you for your search. Below is a checklist you can use to research a company and exercises that will help you gain further perspective on your career interests and summarize your impressions of the workplaces you visit. After you have gathered information from a variety of sources you will begin to see the value of making comparisons.

Research the company

Use the following outline to answer questions that are relevant to your needs. Remember that some companies provide an unusual array of benefits, amenities, and services to employees and are unusually sensitive to employee needs. Research a company you are considering. Compare it with others.

1. Structure
   Divisions
   Locations/length of time there
   Various products and/or services
   Various occupations
   Competitors within the industry as a whole
2. Size
   Number of employees
   Number of locations
   Yearly earnings
3. Performance
   Past history, growth
   Present market

Projections for future development
Reputation/integrity

4. Attitude toward employees
   Benefits:
   Medical/dental
   Life, disability insurance
   Vacations, holidays
   Medical, personal leaves
   Retirement
   Recreation and other personal services
   Profit sharing
   Expenses for moving, travel

   Opportunities:
   Job development counseling
   Merit system
   Promotion or lateral transfers to other jobs/locations

   Education:
   In-service training
   Educational leave
   Workshops

   General employee satisfaction:
   Hours
   Safety hazards

5. Requirements:
   Union membership
   Tools/equipment
   License/certificate

6. Geographical move—consider
   Cost of living:
   Housing
   Food, clothing, other expenses

   Availability of:
   Medical/dental facilities
   Acceptable schools
   Recreational, cultural facilities
   Transportation
   Other amenities

   Disadvantages

Use this list to ask relevant questions at the information or job interview.

Career observation

Here are some questions you might use when you talk to people about careers that interest you.

1. Why did you choose this field?

2. What do you *really* do all day?

3. If you could re-design your job, what parts would you keep and what parts would you get rid of?

4. If you had it to do all over again, what would you have done differently in your career?

5. Whom would you recommend that I interview for a different perspective?

Name _____ Department _____

Company _____ City _____

Phone _____ Extension _____

Important notes:

Summarizing impressions

Describe the workplace you visited:

Location/setting _____

Appearance of buildings:

Outside _____

Work stations _____

Cafeteria _____

Restrooms _____

Equipment _____

Sense impressions:

Colors _____

Light _____

Furnishings (type/arrangement) _____

_____

Odors/sounds _____

_____

General appearance of employees _____

_____

General impressions:

Friendly/not friendly _____

Order/confusion _____

What else? _____

Applying for a job

After you have done a great deal of checking and contacting, you are ready to apply to those places that interest you for the jobs you want. You will need to: (1) check and revise your résumé; (2) write letters, make phone calls; (3) get ready for interviews.

The résumé

A résumé is a summary of data about you that is relevant to the job you seek. Much has been written about the résumé, this sacred cow of the job seeker. Some see it as the most important item to use in presenting oneself; others say preparing a résumé is a worthless exercise. Still, many employers require them, so job hunters, an obliging lot, will continue to oblige.

Some people send a résumé with an individual letter addressed to a specific person in a company. Sometimes the résumé is attached to an application, or requested after an application has been received. The general idea is to give the employer a preview of you, before an interview takes place. Always have your résumé handy, and bring a copy to the interview.

There is no one and only way to write a résumé, but there are some good basic guidelines to follow: (1) be brief, (2) be clear, (3) be neat, (4) be honest. The best résumé describes your qualifications on only one page.

A reasonable résumé should rarely require more than two pages. It should state, succinctly, your education and work experience that specifically relate to the job for which you are applying. It is easiest to read in outline form with plenty of "white space," with good spelling, punctuation, and grammar, and well typed and reproduced. Although it is important to be truthful, a résumé isn't the place for true confessions. Emphasize your good points!

Ask experienced friends to read and criticize your rough draft, but have confidence in your own judgment about what is right for you.

You may spend 12 to 15 hours writing a good résumé, but while you are writing it you will begin to recognize your own qualifications. Start with a separate sheet of paper for each job, project, or volunteer service among your past achieve-

Ideas about résumé form

1. **Name:**
   Address:
   Home phone:
   Business phone:
   (A prospective employer should know where to reach you, day or evening.)

2. **Position objective**

3. **Qualifications in brief**

4. **Experience:**   The order of information may be chronological, functional, or combined.

   Chronological résumé: Beginning with your last job.

   March, 1979: Company, *Job Title*
   June, 1973: Company, *Job Title* (If it seems helpful, add what you *did* very briefly and concisely.) In this type of résumé, you may wish to include a section on community service, military service, or whatever else applies (See pages 119-22.)

   Functional résumé:

   Areas of competence, expertise, or effectiveness, such as public relations, management, organization, program development, sales.

   Follow these by action words like "planned" and "classified," then give summary of the type of things accomplished. You may either list employers and dates briefly at the end or let them appear on the application. (See pages 123-24.)

   Combination of chronological and functional methods:

   This format may suit some individuals' experience; be sure that special skills relevant to a position are highlighted. (See pages 125-26.)

5. **Personal paragraph**

   You may wish to include a statement describing personal attitudes toward your work that make you a valuable and unique employee.

6. **Educational background:**

   The purpose of listing educational background is to indicate general and/or specific training for a job. If a person has little or no educational training, this item is omitted.

   Briefly list
   College: Degrees, major, date, place. If no degrees, give college units completed, major, date, place, or presently attending if this is relevant.
   High school: List diploma if no college attendance.
   Also add: Relevant workshops, adult education, vocational training—either in summary form or chronological order.

Résumé forms

ments. On each sheet, list all the things you did to carry out that activity. Be as detailed as possible so that you won't miss any of your accomplishments.

Then the fun begins. Start sifting, refining, and boiling down until all those pages become one perfect page. It's hard work, but in the process you will get in touch with all the various functions you are able to perform.

Now it is time to decide whether you want a chronological or functional résumé. If your work experience was fairly continuous and can be concisely stated in reverse order, make it chronological. If it was not continuous or consisted of a number of scattered activities or many small jobs, a functional résumé may be best. Perhaps you will want to try both.

Each job involves using *data*, interacting with *people*, or handling *things*—and some jobs require all three. Because you want to tell what you can *do*, you should use action words on your résumé. The following list of action verbs may help you:

Action verb checklist

In the past when using *data*, I have:	Interacting with *people*, I have:	Dealing with *things*, I have:
_____ administered	_____ coordinated	_____ adjusted
_____ analyzed	_____ counseled	_____ altered
_____ compared	_____ directed	_____ assembled
_____ computed	_____ encouraged	_____ balanced
_____ compiled	_____ entertained	_____ built
_____ coordinated	_____ evaluated	_____ driven
_____ designed	_____ instructed	_____ fabricated
_____ developed	_____ interviewed	_____ guided
_____ directed	_____ led	_____ handled
_____ figured	_____ managed	_____ inspected
_____ implemented	_____ motivated	_____ lifted
_____ innovated	_____ negotiated	_____ made
_____ organized	_____ organized	_____ mixed
_____ planned	_____ persuaded	_____ moved
_____ recorded	_____ protected	_____ operated
_____ reported	_____ referred	_____ repaired
_____ researched	_____ served	_____ set up
_____ synthesized	_____ shared	_____ shaped
_____ theorized	_____ supervised	_____ tended
_____ written	_____ trained	_____ tested

Letters of application

Some say that a well-written cover letter is an excellent door opener for an interview. The letter that accompanies your résumé should be brief, clear, neat, and honest. It should be addressed to a specific person, and it may amplify an important aspect of the résumé. Use your cover letter to form a chain linking you to the employer:

Connecting—State your reason for writing and your employment objective. Mention the person who referred you to this employer or the source of the reference, such as a classified ad.

Add more links—State what you can do for the company and why you wish to do it.

Solder the links—Describe your experience in brief and tell how it will help this employer solve his/her problem.

Hold onto the chain—Open the way for the next step by requesting an interview and indicating when you will call to set it up.

After the interview, a letter can be written to thank the interviewer, encourage a reply, request more information, accept or decline an offer.

✳ ✳ ✳ ✳ ✳ ✳ ✳ ✳ ✳ ✳ ✳ ✳

I   A M   R A T H E R
like a mosquito in a nudist
camp; I know what
I ought to do, but I don't
know where to begin.
—STEPHEN BAYNE

✳ ✳ ✳ ✳ ✳ ✳ ✳ ✳ ✳ ✳ ✳ ✳

The following sample résumés and cover letters are those of real job seekers ranging from college student to senior citizen, from engineer to housewife returning to work. Each résumé is unique to one person, as your résumé will be unique to you. But you can use these sample résumés in a number of ways. Notice the variety of forms and styles in the résumés. Select the ones that seem to fit your situation best, and use them as models to create your own unique résumé.

The sample résumés can be used for role playing also. As you read them, pay attention to the person behind the résumé as an interviewer would. Think of questions you might ask the owner of each résumé, and use these questions in mock interviews.

KEVIN DONOVAN
643 Eagle Drive
Dubuque, Iowa 52001

319-555-6789

JOB OBJECTIVE

    CUSTOMER SERVICE - Management Trainee

QUALIFICATIONS IN BRIEF: Learn quickly, easily oriented to job routine.
Possess ability to deal effectively with the public
and flexible enough to work alone or in a team
effort. Good driving record. Not afraid of hard
routine work. Primarily interested in a swing shift
to allow time to further my educational goals.

WORK EXPERIENCE:

    K-MART, Dubuque, IA.   1979 to present
    Customer Service/Bagger

    Help customer with merchandise, stock shelves in warehouse, maintain
appearance of the store, bring carts from parking lot into building,
and bag merchandise from checkstands.

    DUBUQUE GYMNASTIC ASSN., Dubuque, IA.   1978
    Gym Instructor

    Sold memberships and equipment, outlined programs for participants, gave
tours of the facilities to potential customers and guests, balanced
monies and accounts daily, answered phones, and was responsible for maintaining a smoother operation of the gym facilities adding a professional
tone.

    S & S WELDING, East Dubuque, IL.   1977
    VAN'S FURNITURE AND MATTRESS CO., Dubuque, IA.   1976
    Warehouse Worker

    Moved furniture, paint, and equipment, helped with inventory control, and
assisted customers in making proper selections.

EDUCATION:

    LORAS COLLEGE, Dubuque, IA.   1978 to present
    Major: Business/Liberal Arts

    DUBUQUE HIGH SCHOOL, Dubuque, IA.   1974 to 1978
    College Preparatory

REFERENCES: Provided upon request.

Chronological résumé of a college student

AMALIA NIELSON
1643 S. Wildwood Dr.
Fort Lauderdale, FL 33325.
(305) 555-3669

JOB OBJECTIVE:

Manager

QUALIFICATIONS IN BRIEF: High school graduate with concentration in business
courses. Three and one half years experience as bank
teller, preceded by four years of clerical work in a
variety of settings. Extensive community service
activities. Special skills: especially good at business contact with people; fluency in Italian; limited
fluency in Spanish; excellent memory for names.

WORK EXPERIENCE:

CIVIC FEDERAL SAVINGS, Fort Lauderdale, FL.   Present
Head Teller, occasional Acting Manager

Bookkeeping, typing, cashiering, dealing with public at teller window,
paying bank bills. Working with calculator, adding, and NCR machines.
Handling transactions and answering banking questions by phone. As acting
manager, general supervision of personnel and procedures, including
management of vault cash.

DADE COUNTY SANITATION DISTRICT, Miami, FL.   Previous
Office Clerk

Filing, typing, radio communication with personnel in the field, general
telephone work, paying department bills, occasional payroll management.

MIAMI MEDICAL CLINIC, Miami, FL
Medical Records Clerk

Checking for medical records, delivering same to doctors' offices.

ATLANTIC TELEPHONE AND TELEGRAPH, Ft. Lauderdale, FL
Yellow Pages Clerk

WOOLWORTH AND COMPANY, Ft. Lauderdale, FL
Sales Clerk

EDUCATION:

ST. VINCENT'S HIGH SCHOOL, Ft. Lauderdale, FL.
Concentration in business education courses

Subsequent workshops dealing with human relations and crisis counseling.

COMMUNITY SERVICE ACTIVITIES:

Girl Scout/Cub Scout Leader, seven years
Elementary School Teacher
Hospitality Chairperson for PTA Group
Crisis counseling, individually and in small groups

Chronological résumé of a divorced parent returning to the job market

LARRY ANDERSON
32881 Amazon Drive
Silicon Valley, CA 94040   (415) 555-7218

POSITION OBJECTIVE:

Management facilitator of advanced semiconductor products from
design to production.

QUALIFICATIONS IN BRIEF: BSEE and graduate work. Fourteen years of
                            management/engineering experience. Excellent
                            human relations skills.

WORK EXPERIENCE:

ELECTRONIC SYSTEMS, Mountain View, CA   April 1968 to Present
Manager of Manufacturing Engineering

Manage product engineering, instrumentation, and test data processing.

Product Line Manager

Managed transfer of new products from design to production. Directed
yield improvement programs on RAMS and EPROMS.

Instrumentation Manager

Directed personnel, budget, and interdepartmental policies.

Section Head--Instrumentation

Computerized in-house test equipment, both hard and software design.
Supervised assembly groups and electronic stores.

Senior Engineer

Designed and checked all high speed sections of the in-house MOS
test system. Supervised documentation of the complete system.

NATIONAL MICROELECTRONIC DIVISION   May 1965 to Apr. 1968
Supervisor of Instrumentation

Proposed designs for, modified, ordered and maintained test equipment.
Began as junior engineer in device evaluation and became designer of
test equipment of complex MOS IC's.

EDUCATION:

SAN JOSE STATE UNIVERSITY, San Jose, CA
Major: Electrical Engineering BSEE Degree,   1965
        plus sixteen units of graduate work   1965-67

REFERENCES: Provided upon request.

Chronological résumé of a professional engineer

Barbara A. Cline
409 Long Island Drive
College Point, NY 11356

212-555-3600

POSITION OBJECTIVE: Management/Administration
                      Industrial Sales/Development

WORK EXPERIENCE:

FASHION MERCHANDISE WORKERS HEALTH CENTER, New York City, NY   1973-Present
Assistant to Administrative Director

Supervised personnel (165 people in two collective bargaining units),
purchased all supplies, acted as assistant administrator and manager,
coordinated 25 department supervisors, supervised Patient Relations,
Personnel, Printing and Maintenance Departments. Part of management
team that developed and inaugurated an extensive computer system.

NATIONAL CAMPING AND HIKING ASSOCIATION, New York City, NY   1972-1973
Administrative Assistant to Director/Convention Coordinator

Executive secretarial work, bookkeeping, employment referral service,
billing and record keeping for 600 members. Planned and organized
national convention.

GLAMOUR BAG CO., New York City, NY   1971-1972
Secretary to Vice President   Executive level secretarial work.

PRESENCE FREIGHT FORWARDING, New York City, NY   1970-1971
Secretary to Vice President   Secretarial, Bookkeeping.

JUICE AND BEVERAGE MAGAZINE, New York City, NY   1969-1970
Lead/Executive Secretary, Editorial Dept.

Coordinated work and personnel. Prepared manuscripts, did some
research for articles, wrote New Products Section of magazine.

BIO-KEM INSTITUTE, Pittsburgh, PA   1967-1969
Executive Secretary to Vice President for Research and two
research scientists.

Prepared technical manuscripts and federal grant proposals; responsible
for all correspondence. Wrote for and edited in-house newspaper. Handled
details of U.S. Chemical Society Convention.

NATIONAL FEED AND CEREAL CO., Chicago, IL   1965-1967
Executive Secretary to National Sales Manager, Agricultural
Products Division.

PROTECTOR LIFE INSURANCE CO., Chicago, IL   1961-1965
General Clerk, Secretary to Branch Manager

Extensive public contact, coordinated correspondence for 20 agents,
collected money (bonded by National Surety).

PERSONAL QUALIFICATIONS:

Excellent management skills, good organizer, researcher, writer and
editor, experienced at public relations, personnel, purchasing. Have
college credits equivalent to a two year liberal arts degree with a 3.6
average. I am interested in working as part of a dynamic management team.

FASHION MERCHANDISE

WORKERS HEALTH CENTER

100 17th Avenue
New York, NY 10017
212-555-5050

Ms. Margaret Moss, Executive Vice President
Data X Corporation
Silicon Valley, CA 95051

Dear Ms. Moss:

It was enjoyable meeting your interviewer, Jack Smith, at the
Electronics Association Workshop on June 6. I was interested to learn
that your company is developing computer capabilities for use in Health
Maintenance Organization.

I feel that my background would prove helpful in the reorganization
and expansion that you are planning for the Sales and Development Department at Data X. My expertise deals with the way health care is actually
planned for, scheduled and delivered in an outpatient ambulatory care or
HMO setting using computer systems. I have extensive experience in such
areas as doctor and patient appointment scheduling, patient needs and flow,
and statistics. The enclosed resume gives my experience history.

Since I am planning to visit San Francisco this summer, I look
forward to getting together with you to review my qualifications further.
I will call you in about ten days for an appointment.

                                    Sincerely yours,

                                    Barbara A. Cline

**Chronological résumé and cover letter of professional
woman in transition from health care to industry**

GEORGE R. URCIUOLI   (817) 555-6060 (Home)
462 Great Plains Drive
Waco, Texas   (817) 555-2211 (Work)

CAREER OBJECTIVE: Management position in the area of materials planning
and control for manufacturing firm.

CURRENT STATUS: U.S. Army Officer completing 20 years of active duty with
rank of Lt. Colonel.. Leaving military service to start second career in
business.

EXPERIENCE:

MATERIALS CONTROL: Stored and allocated $4.5 million inventory of food,
fuel, ammunition, repair parts, construction material. Coordinated resupply
operation for 22,000 combat troops. Commanded 127 men providing supplies
and services to 2000 combat troops. Directed 90 person team furnishing
materials and electronic instrumentation for R & D project. Implemented
supply and service program for 800 logistics personnel. Scheduled and
coordinated use of ranges, classrooms, training areas, drill fields, test
facilities.

OFFICE ADMINISTRATION: Managed administrative services for command group.
Coordinated projects between senior executives, section chiefs, subordinate
commanders. Participated in forming organizational directorate and organization training center.

HUMAN RELATIONS: As Inspector General, conducted inspections, inquiries,
surveys. Reported allegations, complaints, requests of military personnel
and families. Recommended corrective actions. Advised Commanding General
on activities, attitudes, status of the organization. Performed internal
audits/reviews. Personnel officer for 2,500 person task force.

BUDGETING/ACCOUNTING: As Central Accounting Officer, prepared $1 million
annual budget for Command Sport and Recreation Fund. Administered $600,000
budget for R & D support group. Raised and distributed $20,000 for relief
program. Raised $14,000 for Red Cross drive. Formulated policies and
accounting procedures for various post clubs.

INSTRUCTION: Wrote lesson plans for and conducted weapons training for
18,000 recruits. Directed committee of 104 instructors. Initiated two
training innovations now accepted as standard throughout entire U.S. Army.
Taught management and economics part-time at community college level.

EDUCATION:

BBA 1959 University of the City of New York

MMAS 1974 U.S. Army Command and General Staff College

MBA 1978 Golden Gate University, San Francisco, CA

Functional résumé of a military retiree

```
                    BETTY A. BUG
                 5403 W. Monroe Street
                 Chicago, Illinois   60644
                    312/555-9829


POSITION OBJECTIVE:  Employee trainer in industry

QUALIFICATIONS IN BRIEF:  BA in English, Mundelein College, Chicago, 1973
                          Six years elementary teaching
                          Fluent in Spanish
                          Demonstrated skills in instruction, supervision,
                          communications, human relations.


EXPERIENCE SUMMARY:

  INSTRUCTION:  Planned, organized, presented language and mathematics
  instructional material to elementary students; developed
  instructional modules to solve specific learning problems; developed
  instructional audio-visual material, used audio-visual equipment such
  as overhead, opaque and movie projectors, audio and video cassettes;
  did extensive research in various curricula;  member of curriculum
  development committee;  introduced new motivational techniques for
  students.

  SUPERVISION:  Supervised student groups, teacher interns and a class-
  room aide; evaluated students, peers, and programs; moderated
  student activities.

  HUMAN RELATIONS:  Did effective problem solving/conflict resolution
  between individual students and between student groups;  initiated
  program of student self-governance; acted as liaison between
  families of diverse cultural, ethnic, and economic backgrounds and
  school personnel/services; conducted individual and group conferences
  to establish rapport with parents and discuss student progress.

  COMMUNICATIONS:  Presented new curriculum plans to parent groups;
  sent periodic progress reports to parents; developed class newsletter.

CURRENTLY EMPLOYED:  Austin Elementary School, Chicago, Illinois

REFERENCES:   Provided upon request.
```

Résumé of teacher in transition to industry

Helen B. Bell
432 Spruce Street
Junction City, Kansas 66441
913-555-7035

POSITION OBJECTIVE:

Office Manager with accounting responsibilities.

EXPERIENCE:

Successful Accounting Work: Managed payroll, payroll taxes, accounts receivable, accounts payable, bank reconciliation, and executive credit card expense account; acted as full charge bookkeeper through monthly and annual profit and loss statements.

Supervision and Management: Directed office functions such as secretarial, accounting, customer relations, sales, employee performance and schedules.

EMPLOYERS:

Kindergarten Supplier, USA, Inc., Wichita, KA Accountant	2 years
Electra Corporation, Wichita, KA Receptionist	1 year
Ridgeway Company, Topeka, KA Accountant/Secretary	2 years
Rod's Van & Storage Company, Topeka, KA Accountant/Secretary	2 years
Humphrey Motor Company, Junction City, KA Accountant/Secretary	9 years
Scott Stores, Junction City, KA Bookkeeper	1 year

PERSONAL PARAGRAPH:

The accounting field with its attendant and complex problems is fascinating and thoroughly involving for me. I am interested in insuring smooth flow, efficiency and accuracy of accounts in a moderately sized, growing company.

Functional/chronological résumé of senior citizen/housewife returning to the job market

KATHLEEN M. NEVILLE
791 Peony Lane
Aptos, CA 95003
(415) 555-1730

POSITION OBJECTIVE:

Restaurant Management

QUALIFICATIONS IN BRIEF: AA in Restaurant Management
BA candidate in Business Management
Four years in supervisory capacity
Good human relations skills
Reliable, responsible, creative worker

EDUCATION:

SAN JOSE STATE UNIVERSITY, San Jose, CA   Present
Major: Business Administration

FOOTHILL COMMUNITY COLLEGE, Los Altos Hills, CA 1977
AA Degree in Restaurant Management (Core Courses at West Valley College)

WORK EXPERIENCE:

LINDA'S DRIVE IN, Santa Cruz, CA   August 1974 to Present
Supervisor/Cook

Responsible for daily opening and closing of shop. Inventory, order,
prepare and stock food supplies. Mediate employee and customer problems
and complaints. Train new employees, evaluate employee performance.
Responsible for handling cash, minor repairs.

                                                         Previous

Babysitting and housekeeping throughout junior high and high school.

ACTIVITIES:

GIRL SCOUTS   1964-74

Supervised day camp, planned activities, taught games, arts and crafts,
sports, camping skills and first aid. Solved conflicts. Received art
award.

MUSIC   1966-77

Foothill Youth Symphony, Jazz, Symphony, Marching/Pep Bands at various
times from elementary school through community college. Toured Expo
1974, Spokane, Washington.

DRAMA--AWALT HIGH SCHOOL   1974-75

As Assistant Director made costumes, sets, props.
Performed in Summer Theatre Workshop.

REFERENCES: Provided upon request.

September 17, 1979

Mr. Archibald Manx
The Arrogant Cat
1000 Main Street
Los Gatos, CA 95030

Dear Sir:

Recently it has come to my attention that you have an opening
for a managerial position.

I have had four years supervisory experience working in various
phases of the restaurant business. My intention is to continue in
this field. The excellent quality of The Arrogant Cat, is well known.
I feel that I could be of assistance in maintaining this fine level
of service.

Enclosed is a copy of my resume. I will call you next week for
an appointment to discuss this with you further.

Sincerely yours,
Kathleen M. Neville

791 Peony Lane
Aptos, CA 95003
(415) 555-1730

Chronological résumé and cover letter of a college student

The application

Your application may be the employer's first impression of you. It must look sharp. Carelessness may cause you to be eliminated.

It is essential to fill out an application as clearly, completely, and neatly as possible. Try to obtain two copies ahead of time. (Sometimes companies will mail them to you by phone request.) Type, or at least print, very carefully and completely but succinctly. Keep the extra copy for your file.

Applications vary from one company to another, but what is required essentially is an accurate record of past work experience and education. Prepare a mini-file containing all relevant information. Check it carefully for accuracy.

You will need names, addresses, and dates for both education and work experience. Write for this information if you do not have it. Often these facts are verified, and they should check out. The more careful you are the better you look. Be clear if asked what you did. Know exact job titles, types of machines, salary range, and so on. Here are some helpful hints to remember:

- Read the *whole* application form before beginning to fill it in. Follow all directions, and note the fine print.
- Print with a pen or better still, type answers.
- Fill in all blanks. Use N/A if question does not apply to you.
- You need to obtain a Social Security number if you do not have one. Have it available. Some companies ask for a driver's license as identification. (Revocation or denial of a driver's license can be a clue to some physical or mental problem.)
- Your reason for interest in the position should state advantage to the employer. Research the company and know what you can do for it.
- An arrest is not a conviction. Arrests need not be mentioned.
- Provide accurate names and addresses of those you've contacted who will give you references. Have original reference letters available, plus copies to leave if requested.
- Re-read the application with care.
- Sign the application.

When you apply for a job, the usual procedure in regard to letters of recommendation is to provide them if they are requested or bring copies along to the interview. If letters are on file at a college placement office, have them sent to the employer at this time. But if the competition is fierce and you are almost certain this is a job you want, it may be appropriate to ask a couple of key people to write letters or even make phone calls to the person who may hire you. Ask a teacher or counselor who knows your skills, an acquaintance in the company to which you are applying, or some other professional reference. But understand that this is not the usual procedure and probably should be used with discrimination.

The interview

Although it has been denounced by some as a barbaric custom and by others as "proven ineffectual," the interview is likely to remain an employer ritual for some time to come. Usually an employer interviews persons whose applications, letters, and/or résumés have proven interesting or someone who has made a personal contact or been referred.

An interview is a "structured conversation" between an employer or delegated interviewer and a prospective employee. Its purpose is to exchange information. The interviewer needs to find out if the interviewee has the qualifications necessary to do the job. The applicant needs to make sure he/she understands the job, the company, and what is expected.

The interviewer may be a department head, project director, or even a series of people from various aspects of the job. A group of staff members may act together as an interviewing committee. In a small business you may be interviewed quite casually and briefly by the owner. A large corporation employs professional interviewers. Reputable companies want their interviewers to present a positive image. They want you to leave with a favorable impression of the company, to feel that you were treated well.

Like a good English composition, the interview usually has a beginning, a middle, and an ending. Introductions and casual conversation begin the interview and are designed to help you feel at ease.

After a few minutes most interviewers will guide you to the purpose of the meeting and will then begin inquiries about your qualifications. A good interviewer will also give you information along the way to help you make your decision.

Depending on the level for which you are being considered, an interview might be over in fifteen minutes or last several hours. Most information can be exchanged in thirty to forty-five minutes. Interviewers guide these meetings to an end and usually give information about when you will be notified. They usually are seeing other people, sometimes many others.

An interview is not a time for game-playing or for one person to try to trap the other. It will be counterproductive for both parties if they deceive each other. The interviewer will end up with an employee who "doesn't fit." The worker will be dissatisfied.

However, there are some guidelines you can follow to help you appear at your best. Knowing what to expect ahead of time and preparing well can be important for a successful interview. A successful interview might be one in which you *don't* get the job. In some cases the interview turns up the information that a hire would not be good for either you or the company. In that instance, the interview has accomplished its purpose.

Getting prepared

When you are meeting someone you wish to impress, common sense and courtesy are your most reliable guides. Lean slightly toward the conservative in dress and

manner if you have any doubts along this line. A genial, positive, low-keyed
manner and sense of humor are valuable assets. Generally let the interviewer set the pace and "be in charge." Don't try to take over unless the situation clearly calls for tactful assertion (for example, if you have had little chance to state your abilities).

The very best preparation for the interview is practice. Practice talking to people about their jobs; practice calling for appointments to see people in order to ask for career information. Go on interviews even if you think you might not get a job, and then honestly assess your performance.

More immediately, do homework on the company you are approaching. Many have brochures; many are listed in standard library references. A call to the public relations department can sometimes result in a wealth of material. Talk to people, ask questions. Try to see how you best fit in. Know the important facts about the job and, if possible, the salary range. Prepare to bring any relevant examples of your work, such as sketches, designs, writings.

In some career areas, salaries are nonnegotiable and not an issue—the teaching profession and unions are such examples. In others they *are* negotiable. In such cases the interviewer may ask what salary you expect. If you have no idea of the range and were not able to find out ahead of time, ask. Unless you are a superstar, don't ask for the top of the range, but don't undervalue yourself either. Place yourself somewhere in the middle and leave it open to negotiation. Also, you might ask for a salary review in six months or so.

Don't be afraid to ask about salary and benefits such as medical, dental, disability, and life insurance, vacations, and retirement plans if these are vitally important. A better way is to check all this out before the interview. Ask the personnel office for brochures on their benefit plans. Also feel free to ask when you will hear the results of the interview if you aren't told.

Follow up the interview with a thank-you letter and then a phone call after a week or so if there is no word—unless you have been given a different time line.

Areas of emphasis

As part of your interview, you may be asked questions about your likes, dislikes, and opinions. The questions asked and the answers you give will depend on your experience and the type of job and company. The interviewer is trying to find out if you have reflected on important aspects of your life as it may affect your work, and if you can talk about them easily.

Be prepared for questions about the following subjects:

Work experience
   Major responsibilities
   General impressions of the company
   Successes
   Problems

Progress and self-development
Use of your ability
Supervisors
Attendance
Reasons for leaving

Education
Courses
Reasons for choice of major
Instructors
Activities, clubs, offices held
Financing

Military experience

Yourself and your values
Strengths, weaknesses
Service to others
Money
Work values
alone/with others
close supervision/on your own
regular/variable hours/overtime
routine/varied work
large/small company
travel
physical/mental activity

Family life
Parents
Spouse
Children

Leisure
Friends
Hobbies and recreation
Books, magazines, TV
Vacations and travel

Goals for the future
Position
Growth/development
Salary
Location of work
Lifestyle you envision

Interview behavior

As a job seeker, you should approach each interview by being yourself, being true to yourself, and trusting your own judgment about the style that suits you best. Perhaps you can build self-confidence by practicing ways of talking and listening effectively and by learning to answer an interviewer's questions. Here are some key points to practice.

Good eye contact: Don't avoid this form of personal contact. If you like your interviewers, your eyes will communicate warmth and liking.

Appropriate body language: Be relaxed and open, interested and attentive. Notice how bodies speak! Become aware of ways in which your body sends messages of boredom, fear, enthusiasm, cockiness, nervousness, confidence.

Appropriate voice melody: Try to come across with vitality, enthusiasm, and confidence. Remember that low tones convey confidence and competence, high tones convey insecurity.

Active listening: Indicate that you have heard and understood what the interviewer has said. For example, if the interviewer mentions tardiness as a problem, say, "It must be difficult to have employees who are late all the time. I can assure you that I'll be on time."

Good choice of words: If you do your interview homework and practice, the right words should come easily. Much of what you "say" will of course be conveyed by your manner, not your words.

Practice questions

Questions dealing with factual information should not be a problem if you have done your homework. Have on hand your own file of all education, previous jobs, and other experience, with correct dates, place names and addresses, job titles and duties, names of supervisors and other relevant information in case these might slip your mind. Usually this information is on the application. The interview centers around clarification of points on the application and résumé.

If you have been working regularly and successfully in your field for a period of years, this part of the interview will be mainly a chance for you to tell what you have done. If you are a young graduate, this discussion may center around your education, interests, and casual jobs.

If you have been in and out of the job market or have had some past problems, the interviewer will want to explore the reasons. Be relaxed and not defensive. Look upon this as a chance to make a fresh start. You will need to assure the interviewer that you will not be a *problem*, but a *solution*!

Here are some typical questions, along with answers for you to consider.

Why did you leave your last job? People leave jobs for many reasons. Some replies could be:

- ■ "I seemed to have reached a point where there was little potential for growth."

- "I have learned my job well and would like to try new dimensions of it in a growing (or larger, or innovative) company."
- "I decided to change careers, and I just got my degree in . . ."
- "I left to raise a family and now I am ready to return to work permanently."

In your previous jobs over the past years you've been doing much the same thing. Now you are applying for a higher level position (or a different career). Can you explain why? Perhaps you have just now completed course work, finished raising children, or come to new realizations about your ability. Be aware of what has prompted you, after all these years, to "get ahead" or to "make a change."

Your application indicates that you have been in and out of the work force quite often (or haven't worked in some years). What were you involved with in those periods of unemployment? Here the interviewer has several concerns. One is that you might be likely to leave after being trained for this job. Another is that your skills might be rusty. Be prepared to give assurance that you plan to stay with this job and that your qualifications are such that you can handle it. Knowing your abilities and what the job demands can clarify this subject for you.

Why do you think you would like to work for our company? When most individuals look for a job, they are more interested in getting a good job than in being particular about where they work. It comes across that they don't care about the company. One of the most important things you should do before you go to an interview, or ask for one, is find out all you can about the company. Identify some positive things about policies, procedures, or products that you can discuss with interest. Do your homework—so that you will have work to come home from.

In what type of position are you most interested? Tell them what kind of function you like—such as "I am good at accounting and math," then name positions related to these skills, such as accounts payable. Give the employer an opportunity to put you where you fit best, by being able to tell what you do best, not just your last job title. But avoid too eager discussion of your desire for advanced positions.

Imagined situations that test a person's knowledge of the job may begin with questions like, "What would you do if . . ." The quality of your solution is not nearly as important as your attitude. A calm approach is a best bet. It's better to cushion your statements with answers like, "One of the things I might consider would be . . ." If you commit yourself to a process of what you *would* do, and it isn't one *they* would like or consider, you are in an awkward position. Give your answer a cushion of several possible choices.

How did you get along with . . . This question can be asked regarding supervisors, co-workers or subordinates, or even teachers. If you generally get along with people, say so. If you had a problem with someone, there is usually no need here to tell the whole tale. Simply say that occasionally you've had to work out difficulties with people. Be positive, not blaming or complaining.

Do you have any physical limitations that may interfere with your performance? If you do not, there is no problem. If you *do* have a physical limitation or a past history of serious illness, be prepared to show that it will not interfere with your work. A doctor's statement might be helpful here.

Are you looking for a full-time or part-time job? If you can be placed immediately only in part-time work, then working part-time may be good for you until the company can hire you on a full-time basis. Employers are more inclined to hire for full-time from a part-time employment pool than to take a person from the outside.

Tell me something about yourself. This question could be followed by a dismayed silence as you race your mental motor trying to find something to talk about. If you are prepared, you will hop in happily with the reasons you feel that your skills, background, and personal attitudes are good for the job and how you see your future with the company. You will seldom have a better opportunity than this to tell about yourself.

What are your weaknesses, and what are your strengths? Smile when they ask this one. Have a list that you have memorized about what you do best, such as "I work well with other people on a team basis." Then make your weaknesses possible strengths—for instance, "One of my weaknesses is that I find it hard to release responsibility, so frequently I spend a lot of time doing the job myself."

We have many qualified applicants. Why do you think we should hire you for this job? One of the best approaches here is to convey that you are not in a position to evaluate the other candidates, but you can answer well about yourself. You believe that your background, experience, and interest in the job equip you to handle the work well. It is important to say "believe" because the truth is until you do the job, you won't actually *know* how well you can do it. Remember, they can argue facts, but they can't argue with your feelings. If you say you feel or believe you can do the work, you are being believably honest.

How long do you expect to work for us? The bald truth is that a company will not keep employees past their ability to use their skills. And you are not going to work for a company past the time that it is good for you. The best answer might be, "As long as it is good for both of us."

Do you have any questions about the company or the job? Employers, down at the bottom of their company hearts, believe the myth that good people are hard to find. If asked, a good person is always one that is really interested in the company and in the job that they do. So this is an ideal time to relate your interest, enthusiasm, and commitment to the company and the job.[2]

Questions to resolve honestly ahead of time:

Are you willing to/can you
> move (or travel)?
> work overtime?
> take a temporary job?

Do you have plans for
> your next job?
> your next few years?
> starting your own business?
> changing fields?

Sometimes you may be asked questions that startle you. If you feel unprepared, it's wise to say, "I need a few moments to think about that." Then take a few deep breaths, relax, and begin confidently. If it should happen that you still "draw a blank," be prepared to deal with the situation. Possibilities: "Maybe we could come

HERMAN *by Unger*

I've got two other applicants to see before I make my final choice.

INTERVIEW RATING

CONFIDENTIAL

UNIVERSITY OF SANTA CLARA
CAREER PLANNING AND PLACEMENT OFFICE

FIRM: _____

RECRUITER: _____   DATE: _____

I. CHARACTERISTICS OF CANDIDATE:
    A = Interview preparation
    B = Clarity of career objectives
    C = Realistic career objectives
    D = Appropriate academic preparation
    E = Personal appearance
    F = Communicative ability
    G = Emotional maturity
    H = Self-confidence
    I = Motivation
    J = Overall rating

II. EMPLOYER INTEREST:
    1 = Particularly high interest
    2 = Interest with further consideration necessary
    3 = Prefer not to make offer
    4 = Need placement counseling

III. ADDITIONAL COMMENTS:

RATING SCALE: 1) Outstanding   2) Above average   3) Average   4) Below average   5) Poor

NAME	I. CHARACTERISTICS OF CANDIDATE										II.	III. COMMENTS
	A	B	C	D	E	F	G	H	I	J		

SAMPLE
This is an interview rating form used by campus recruiters. Note the characteristics that some interviewers may find important. You may wish to use it to rate members of a group role-playing the interview.

back to that later," or "I really should be prepared to answer that but I'm not." It's a learning experience, and you learn that you can keep cool.

Know your successes and failures, your strengths and weaknesses. Be prepared for some difficult ("Whew!") questions if you have ever been convicted of a crime or fired for serious problems, or if you have a poor work record. Take a deep breath, relax a minute, look at the interviewer, and say in your own words something like this: "Yes, I made a mistake [or have done poorly in the past] but I learned my lesson, and I'm determined that it won't happen again."

Perhaps you can include some recent experience as evidence that you've made some changes in your life. Again, you need to reassure the interviewer that you are capable of doing the job.

You might be startled by inappropriate questions that appear to have nothing to do with job qualifications, or even illegal questions that indicate job discrimination. The interviewer should not ask questions about age, race, religion, nationality, or handicaps unless the answers are job-related. Also inappropriate are questions that discriminate between males and females, for example, questions about family planning, child care, or pregnancy. Even questions about education may be discriminatory if not related to job performance.

Decide in advance how you will answer such questions if they are asked. If the issue is not really important, you might prefer to answer the question rather than risk alienating the interviewer with a refusal. If you'd prefer not to answer, you might say, "I wasn't aware that this was a requirement for the job," or, "Can you explain how this question relates to the job?" One can appeal to the law in obvious cases of prejudice; in less serious instances, a good sense of humor and respect for others can be enormously helpful.

After you are hired, you may be asked to supply such items as a birth certificate, proof of citizenship, a photograph, and proof of age. Have these items ready if you feel they might be required.

Job offers: Too many or too few?

You probably will not get a job offer during your first interview. In competitive fields, people interview for many months before they find jobs. But suppose you get a job offer—or two or three—in this early phase of your career search. Maybe you had planned to do personnel work, but the welding shop would welcome you! Beware of such decisions. You can easily get carried away with excitement and leap into the first job that comes along.

Some jobs sound rewarding in terms of personal growth opportunities, but the salary is so low you could not live on it without making sacrifices. Another job pays very well, but the work sounds dull and disagreeable. You might even be offered a temporary job; it would fulfill your immediate needs, but you'd be back on the job

Interview Overview

☞ GET READY

CHECK: The company (from reference section of library, public relations department of firm, friends)

Its locations
Products and services
Potential market
Earnings
Policies
How/where do you fit in?
What else?

CHECK: Important items you wish to cover

Your strengths
Your experiences
Your interests

☞ GET SET

CHECK: Items for application (if to be filled out there)

Social Security number
Address, phone number
Employers and dates
Supervisors' names
Schools, dates
Perso. to notify in case of accident
Military information
References (usually three—not family—and with their permission; originals plus copies of letters)

CHECK: Copies of résumé, letters of reference, and if relevant, examples of work

Exact time, date, location (building and room), parking

Name of interviewer (and its pronunciation)
Go alone

☞ GO

CHECK: Your appearance:

Neat, clean, conservative outfit
No gum, no smoking, no fidgeting
Sit comfortably, straight, at ease

Your attitude: a serious job seeker

Definite goals
Willing to work and work up
Reasonable approach to salary, hours, benefits or other aspects of the job
Uncritical of past employers, teachers, co-workers
Evidence of good human relations
Sense of humor
High personal values
Wide interests, openness, flexibility

Your manner:

Confident, not overbearing
Enthusiastic but not desperate or gushy
Courteous, attentive
Good voice, expression
On target answering questions
Shake hands firmly
Leave promptly after interview

market in six months or so. Should you accept one of these less desirable jobs just to get hired or to get experience?

Now is the time to review your needs, wants, and values and become very clear about what it is that you want the job to do. Perhaps your goal is just to get into a special company that you've chosen. Taking a job you don't particularly like could give you this chance. Many companies promote from within before they open jobs to outsiders.

If you aren't hired for the job you really want right away, you may be only one of many well-qualified applicants. In a competitive field it can take six months or more of continuous job hunting to find a job. Whether you should take a less desirable job depends on how long you can afford to wait and continue the search. If you job-hunt for many months without a nibble, you may need to consider alternatives: other careers, new training, other opportunities in your present position, additional paid or volunteer experience that might be useful in a different kind of job.

 **EXERCISES:**   THE JOB HUNT

1. Begin your résumé here

   Begin getting practice here with a rough draft of some items you might use on your résumé.

Name
Address
Phone

Job objective: _____

_____   _____

Qualifications in brief: _____

_____

Experience: _____

_____

_____

_____

_____

Education: _____

_____

_____

Personal paragraph: _____

_____

_____

_____

_____

_____

Follow this with any items of special note, such as honors, work published, organizational membership. Avoid trivia here.

Be prepared to supply the names of people who have written or will write letters of reference for you (with their permission). These should be professional people, former employers—preferably people who are acquainted with your work skills. Some college placement offices will keep references, a current résumé, and transcripts on file for their graduates and will send them out to prospective employers for a nominal fee.

2. Write a cover letter to accompany your résumé.

3. Fill out the sample application that follows.

HEWLETT **hp** PACKARD
1501 Page Mill Road, Palo Alto, California 94304

EMPLOYMENT APPLICATION

HEWLETT-PACKARD IS AN EQUAL OPPORTUNITY EMPLOYER AND ALL APPLICANTS ARE WELCOME.

PERSONAL INFORMATION

NAME: _____   Social Security No.: _____ — — _____
  Last   First   Middle

Address: _____
  No.   Street   City   State   Zip

Telephone No. _____ Message No. (If necessary): _____
  (Area Code)   Number   (Area Code)   Number

Other name(s) under which you have worked: _____

Have you ever applied for employment at HP?:   Yes ☐   No ☐   If "yes", Location: _____   Date: _____

Previously employed with HP?:   Yes ☐   No ☐   If "yes", Location: _____   Date: _____

Names of relatives employed here: _____   Relationship: _____   Location at HP: _____

How were you referred to HP? _____

If not a U.S. citizen, please name type of visa: _____

Have you ever been convicted of a felony?: Yes ☐   No ☐   If "yes", give date, place, offense, and outcome: _____

_____
Previous convictions do not exclude an applicant from consideration for employment.

Are you between the ages of 18 and 70? Yes ☐   No ☐. All applicants under the age of 18 must submit a work permit.

TYPE OF WORK APPLYING FOR

CHECK:
☐ Electronic Tech. ☐ Machinist ☐ Tech. Maint. ☐ Stock ☐ Custodian
☐ Shop Helper ☐ Computer Op. ☐ Assembly ☐ Office ☐ Other _____

State specific type of job in the area you checked and your qualifications: _____

_____

Shift(s):   Day _____   Swing _____   Grave _____   Hours: Full-time _____   Part-time _____

Do you have any physical condition which may limit your ability to perform the job(s) applied for? ☐ Yes   ☐ No

OFFICE	SHOP	OTHER
Typing Speed _____ WPM	List tools and machines you feel qualified to use without further experience.	What specific skills or abilities do you have?
Shorthand Speed _____		_____
Office Machines _____	_____	_____
	_____	_____
Keypunch/Data Proc.: _____	_____	_____

EDUCATION

CIRCLE LAST GRADE COMPLETED — Grade 1 2 3 4 5 6 7 8 9 10 11 12   College   1 2 3 4

Name(s) of School(s) other than high school: Location   Major   Dates   Degree (if any)

_____

_____

_____

Is there anything else you would like us to know about you? _____

_____

US MILITARY

BRANCH	LAST RANK	DATE OF SEPARATION

Your most important duties and training during service: (include schools attended) _____

_____

WORK EXPERIENCE

LIST PREVIOUS JOBS STARTING WITH YOUR PRESENT OR MOST RECENT ONE. PLEASE DESCRIBE DUTIES AS COMPLETELY AS SPACE ALLOWS.

Present or
Last Employer: _____

Reason for Leaving: _____

Dates Start	Salary Start
/ /	$
Left	Left

Address: _____
Number   Street

_____

/ /	$

City   State   Zip

Telephone No.: _____
(Area Code)   Number

Supervisor: _____

Your Duties: _____

Employer: _____

Reason for Leaving: _____

Dates Start	Salary Start
/ /	$
Left	Left

Address: _____
Number   Street

_____

/ /	$

City   State   Zip

Telephone No.: _____
(Area Code)   Number

Supervisor: _____

Your Duties: _____

Employer: _____

Reason for Leaving: _____

Dates Start	Salary Start
/ /	$
Left	Left

Address: _____
Number   Street

_____

/ /	$

City   State   Zip

Telephone No.: _____
(Area Code)   Number

Supervisor: _____

Your Duties: _____

Employer: _____

Reason for Leaving: _____

Dates Start	Salary Start
/ /	$
Left	Left

Address: _____
Number   Street

_____

/ /	$

City   State   Zip

Telephone No.: _____
(Area Code)   Number

Supervisor: _____

Your Duties: _____

REFERENCES

One of HP's pre-employment steps is to contact your previous employers.
May we contact your present employer?   ☐ Yes   ☐ No

IN THE SPACE BELOW PLEASE LIST PERSONAL REFERENCES WHO CAN COMMENT ON YOUR EDUCATIONAL OR JOB RELATED EXPERIENCE: (DO NOT GIVE RELATIVES OR YOUR EMPLOYERS LISTED ABOVE)

NAME _____   PHONE NO. — 8AM—5 PM

NAME _____   PHONE NO. — 8AM—5 PM

NAME _____   PHONE NO. — 8 AM—5 PM

LOCA-TION

PLEASE CHECK LOCATIONS WHERE YOU ARE WILLING TO WORK:

☐ Palo Alto   ☐ Cupertino   ☐ Mountain View   ☐ Santa Rosa
☐ Santa Clara   ☐ San Jose   ☐ Sunnyvale

SIGNATURE

THIS APPLICATION IS NOT COMPLETE UNTIL THE FOLLOWING STATEMENT HAS BEEN READ AND SIGNED:
I certify that all of the information furnished on this form is true, complete, and correct to the best of my knowledge. I understand that such information is subject to verification by Hewlett-Packard.

_____   _____
SIGNATURE   DATE

EMPLOYMENT OFFICE COMMENTS

_____

_____

_____

DISPOSITION OF APPLICATION:

Post Card _____   RLC
           Date   Date   126

Seven — Decisions, decisions:

What's your next move?

Where are you *now* on your career choice continuum? Each person begins the career search process at a different point and travels at a different speed. In a career course, some students make choices during the first few weeks, but others are still undecided after the last class is over. Perhaps you are still uneasy about your career decision. Do you view several careers with equal enthusiasm? Should you go back to school? Do you feel you should change your approach, rather than your career? Should you keep your present job? Or decide not to decide for awhile? Perhaps you need to improve your ability to make decisions.

As an aid to decision-making, for example, you might narrow down the number of alternatives you're trying to deal with. Instead of trying to consider 66 job groups, think in terms of workplaces. In those terms there are only seven choices, because there are seven general types or categories of workplaces: business, industry, education, entertainment/communication, health, government, and military. Let's look at each of these broad categories.

Business includes every desk from an executive suite to a tiny space in the back of an auto repair shop. Business is not limited to office buildings: it occurs wherever two or more people get together to trade goods or services. Its workers range from the retail clerks in your neighborhood record shop to the shipping tycoon who has private offices around the world, from one person working at home to a complex international organization. Labor relations, personnel, contract negotiations, consulting, accounting, marketing, and hundreds of other functions make up the work of the business world, and the secretarial pool is one of its many support systems.

The Enterprising and Conventional Types are most at home in business, but all types can find expression here: the social personality in dealing with people and their problems, the artistic person in advertising or creating new designs, the realistic in handling products and production, and the investigative in research and

143

problem-solving. Choosing business, then, will narrow down your choices yet leave the door open to a variety of careers.

To facilitate the flow of goods and services, business involves paper: writing it, reading it, typing it, data/word processing it, and filing it. General clerical skills will enable you to enter the field of business in positions such as filing or shipping clerk. When you feel the need for more training, you can attend workshops and seminars or take college work at the A.A. or B.A. level. Or you might go directly to college to earn a B.A. in Business, in a field such as accounting or management. Even with a B.A. degree, however, most people must start near the bottom of the ladder and work up—unless there is a serious shortage of personnel.

Industry can be defined loosely as a concern with products, not with people or paper (if you exclude the "business end" of industry). Repairing cars, pouring concrete, and raising wheat are industries in this sense. Even the artist making clay pots at home is involved in industry. Working with machines and tools and tangible materials attracts the realistic person to industries of all kinds.

Education offers many careers besides teaching in schools and colleges. Computer companies hire specialists to develop learning programs, while business and industry carry on employee training programs of all sorts. People who teach cooking or carfts at home or at community centers are also part of education.

The enterprising and social personalities enjoy the task-oriented interaction of teaching, leading, and motivating others. Realistic personalities enjoy teaching such subjects as physical education and shop, while the artistic types drift toward fine arts, crafts, and design classes. Investigative interests are needed for scholarship and research, while conventional personalities do well in teaching "the basics." In fact, all personality types can be found in education—it helps to be a "jack of all trades" when teaching.

Entertainment/communication ranges from circus tents to TV studios, but its opportunities tend to be more limited than those in any other area because it is highly competitive. In order to succeed here, you need exceptional ability, great quantities of luck, and lots of courage. Artistic personalities are naturally attracted to entertainment and communication but may be unsuccessful unless they possess some of the qualities of the Enterprising Type (or possibly a good agent).

Health suggests a hospital or a doctor's office, but in fact health care workers find employment also in business, industry, schools, and military settings. The investigative person with a good social orientation will enjoy the challenge of helping people solve their health care problems. This area is expanding rapidly as specialization trends and technological advances continue. There are several hundred job titles involved in the delivery of health care.

Government is employing more and more people of all types in every variety of setting from agricultural stations to hospitals. One must usually pass a "test" to become employed at the federal level (and often at state and county levels, too). The test may combine an oral interview and a written examination with points added for years of education, military service, and past work experience. Any type of personality can find satisfiers on one or another of the vast array of government jobs.

Traditionally, a government job implied security but low pay. In recent years the pay has increased, along with the number of jobs. But now the taxpayers' mood seems to be moving against this trend. If the mood prevails, low pay and insecurity may result for employees of the government.

Military operations and procedures appeal most readily to realistic and conventional personalities, but here again, people of all types can find opportunities of many varieties, from cooking to hospital laboratory work to sophisticated industrial research and design. For those so inclined, the military provides a good living with training in a variety of skills.

And finally, some people conclude that no job in existence will give them enough of their satisfiers. They decide to create their own careers to serve an unmet need in society. You may be one of these creative folk.

Which of these categories seems to fit you? Choosing a workplace focuses your career exploration and can even get you started on a basic curriculum.

Back to school

You may wish to take additional courses to improve your basic language and math skills, to explore various majors, to prepare for possible careers, or just to foster personal enrichment and growth. Do not let your age or your previous school record discourage you. A recent newspaper article pictured a man of 92 receiving his Associate of Arts degree. Many returning students have previous school records that qualify as disasters, but now, because they are mature and motivated, they can reach their goals. So can you.

If your high school education was incomplete or deficient, consider basic skill courses in language and math at community colleges or adult education centers. Usually counselors are available to help you decide which courses to take. Search for someone who understands exactly where you are now, and how you feel about it.

A two-year community college (junior college) is a good place to explore various majors. Obtain a catalog and look for introductory courses. The titles of these courses frequently include terms such as *Beginning, Orientation to, Introduction to,* or *Principles of.* The catalog will tell you the required courses and general degree requirements for each major. Usually advisors or counselors will be available to help you through the maze of choices.

If you want a college degree at the four-year level, you can go directly to a four-year institution, or you can attend a community college for two years and then transfer to a four-year college or university to complete your junior- and senior-level courses. The four-year "package" can be outlined as follows:

First year: Exploring majors, general education (GE), and electives
Second year: Major requirements, GE, and electives
Third year: Major requirements, electives, and remaining GE
Fourth year: Major requirements and electives

You will probably need more math if you are interested in science, four-year business or technical field, architecture, or engineering. The usual sequence is as follows:

High school: Arithmetic, introductory algebra, plane geometry, intermediate algebra, trigonometry, college (pre-calculus) algebra or "senior math"
College: College algebra, calculus (two to three semesters or five quarters), other advanced courses as needed and required

First, check to see how much math you need for various programs. (You may not need any at all.) Then try to start where you left off or where you feel most comfortable. Before you try to enroll in a course, however, find out whether you must complete any prerequisites; a *prerequisite* is an elementary course that you need in order to be eligible for enrollment in a more advanced course.

Adult education programs offer math courses at the high school level and possibly beyond. Community colleges offer not only high school level courses but also most of the college courses at the freshman and sophomore level.

You can find courses for personal growth and enrichment in colleges, adult education programs, and community centers. Many are noncredit courses, which provide an easy way to start back to school.

If returning to school seems impossible—because of distance, for example—investigate tutoring services, correspondence courses, and courses by TV. Some colleges and universities administer tests like the College Level Entry Program (CLEP), which enable you to earn credit by examination. Some give credit for work experience. You may be required to attend the school in order to receive credit by examination or through work experience, but such credits decrease the time that you need to spend on campus.

If finances are a problem, apply for financial aid. Sometimes students of all ages can get grants and low-interest loans for education. Some people change their life-styles, mortgage or sell their houses, sell their cars and ride a bike.

Remember, too, that much learning takes place off campus. You can teach yourself many things, and you can find others who will help you learn. Much depends on having a goal and working toward it—or being flexible enough to see alternatives.

Remember that most jobs require only average to somewhat above average skills. Talking to people "in the field" can help you to assess your motivation to go on with it, especially if it looks as though you'll need years of training. Remember, however, when you meet a competent professional all trained, experienced, and "'way up there," it wasn't done in one step. Most valuable in acquiring high-level ability is the patience to stay with it until you learn it. But hard work is fun if you are doing what you enjoy.

As you go along, new horizons will open up. You can also float to your level. Before the end of your training, you may choose to stop out at a point where you feel comfortable. Instead of going straight on to become a certified public accountant, for example, you might try work experience as an accounting clerk, which might lead you in a direction that you hadn't seen before.

You may find along the way that you'd like to float sideways to a different area with similar satisfiers. The more homework you've done regarding your interests, the more quickly you'll be able to make such changes.

If you simply must get more detailed information about your skills, your aptitudes to develop skills, or where your skills need sharpening, you can contact a counselor at a local college, state employment office, or in private practice. You can arrange to take such tests as the DAT (Differential Aptitude Test) or the GATB (the General Aptitude Test Battery).

Same job—new approach

If you are already employed, a brief exploration of the job market may convince you that your present job isn't so bad after all. "Then why," you will wonder, "do I feel dissatisfied?" A most common explanation is, "I'm not comfortable with my co-workers." Often communications problems are at the root of this discomfort. Would some fine tuning in human relations improve your work life?

You may wish to check these items: Are you pleasant and easy to get along with? Do you overlook other people's minor shortcomings? Do your appearance and manner fit in with the style of your workplace? Do you give others credit and praise?

If your job is beginning to call for new duties, such as public presentations or writing, some of your basic skills may need improving. Try to put energy into your job, and to learn as much as you can in order to grow and develop. Your self-confidence will improve along with your skills.

Amazingly, some people are so successful they are promoted beyond the level of their own self-confidence. Suddenly they discover that everyone believes in them except themselves. If you are unhappy with yourself, consider enrolling in some growth classes—or at least do some reading in the area of personal growth. If a problem is weighing on you, discuss it with a trusted friend or a counselor. Many problems have obvious solutions that we miss when searching alone.

But there is no magic formula for career success. Perhaps you've improved your skills—including your human relations skills—and solved the problems that stood in the way of your personal growth. Still your job doesn't seem to be working out well, so you (or your employer) decide to call it quits. Suddenly you are jobless and worried about where to go next. But you are also sleeping-in some mornings, catching up on errands, enjoying an occasional walk on the beach. That's good: the more you can enjoy your new leisure, the better you'll be able to plan your next step. Be open to new ideas at times like this.

Some questions you need to answer are: Do I want to do almost exactly the same job in a similar setting? Do I want to get out of the old line of work or into another type of workplace? Do I want to make a career change, create my own career, start a new business, go back to school? Most important, what changes can I make in myself to put me in harmony with my choices? What skills did I learn and develop on my last job? Did that job put me in touch with new interests? What did I dislike about that job?

If you were fired or laid off, evaluate the causes to see how they can be avoided in the future. Ask for help from friends, relatives, and neighbors without hiding your job loss. As everyone knows, it can happen to anyone. Despite the very real trauma involved in being jobless, you can use the experience to advantage by preparing for your next job: Learn to pick up cues that will help you to make changes or seize opportunities *before* you are laid off or fired. Keep up contacts and keep other options open, instead of sinking into mindless security on your job. You can't always plan your career step by step, but you can adopt a game plan that provides alternatives.

Deciding not to decide

When you keep the status quo, you are deciding not to decide—which can be a good decision. You might stay in the same job, take more classes, or continue to be at home with your children. You may need to do more exploring and evaluating, but try to set a time limit, say six months to a year.

Assessing the risks

Bear in mind that any change involves a risk. Without a crystal ball, it's hard to predict exactly how a decision is going to work out. Even the most carefully reasoned and promising decision can bring disappointing results. In such cases, try to avoid blaming yourself, but give yourself credit for having taken the risk.

Some decisions that won't work result in lost time and money, or even physical injury. But many risks involve merely the approval of others: What will people

think? Indeed, you may find yourself preserving the status quo solely out of fear of others' opinions. If so, you're giving others a great deal of power over your life. There is no way to change and grow without some risk. And for those of you who are faint-hearted, it is important to learn to take that tiny first step.

Every change, even if it's only re-arranging the garage, has an impact on others. Caring for those around you involves bringing them along with your decision-making, that is, communicating your own needs honestly while listening to theirs, keeping them informed as you make changes. Hardly any change is perfect. There will be advantages and disadvantages to most moves. The idea is to *maximize the advantages*.

HERMAN *by Unger*

Pssst, boss. I guess this is not a good time to ask for a raise, huh?

Copyright 1976
Universal Press Syndicate

It may be helpful to look at your decision-making style before plunging into the excitement of change. See if it needs a "tune-up" to facilitate your choices. Then analyze things that need deciding in your life and decide the steps you'll take to carry out your goals. Give yourself a "getting employed" time line, along with a clear list of the minimum characteristics you would accept in a job.

If you are still unable to choose a career, select one type of workplace to explore. Find out whether your skills are needed and appreciated in this particular environment. When you know your skills are needed, you have the confidence to take action. When you believe in yourself as a capable person, you are on your way to further growth and self-fulfillment. The steps you take create your life.

Remember that you, and only you, have the ability to make your decisions and take responsibility for them. You make many decisions every day. It's helpful to reflect on how you do it.

1. Making decisions

I make decisions:	Always	Sometimes	Never
1. After considering many alternatives			
2. Easily, without undue agonizing			
3. Based on information			
4. Based on feeling			
5. I take responsibility for the consequences of my decisions (clearing up the fall-out)			
6. I make my own decisions, not shifting responsibility to others			
7. I consult with others, but my decisions are my own			
8. I compromise when the needs of others are involved			
9. I make some decisions to fulfill my own needs			
10. I "test out" major decisions ahead of time where possible			
11. If a decision doesn't work, I try another plan			

2. Making changes

If you are still clarifying your decisions, make a list of "things that need deciding" in the left-hand column below. Rate the degree of risk as LO, MED, or HI, and mention some possible outcomes, both positive and negative. For example:

	Risk			Possible results	
	LO	MED	HI	+	−

Skills

Improve human relations skills

		✓		*Move into management*	*Risk failure*
				Better salary/status	*More pressures*

Family

Relocate family

		✓		*Promotion*	*Family resistance*
				New challenges	*Loss of friends*
				Better salary	*Change of schools*

	Risk			Possible results	
	LO	MED	HI	+	−

Career

Education

| | Risk | | | Possible results | |
Skills	LO	MED	HI	+	−
Family					
Housing					
Food/clothing					
Social life & friends					
Other					

3. Goal selection

Select three to five of the goals listed in Exercise 2 that are most important to you. State, as specifically as possible, all the steps you would need to take and could take to accomplish these changes. Are you willing to make a time line indicating approximately how soon you would like to accomplish these changes and related steps? Are your goals realistic? Do they harmonize with your values?

Changes		Steps	Realistic?	Value related?
1. _____	a.			
_____	b.			
_____	c.			
_____	d.			
_____	e.			
2. _____	a.			
_____	b.			
_____	c.			
_____	d.			
_____	e.			
3. _____	a.			
_____	b.			
_____	c.			
_____	d.			
_____	e.			
4. _____	a.			
_____	b.			
_____	c.			
_____	d.			
_____	e.			

Changes		Steps	Realistic?	Value related?
5. _____	a.			
_____	b.			
_____	c.			
_____	d.			
_____	e.			

Time line

Date: _____   Date: _____

Now   *Then*

4. Categories of workplaces

Pick one (or more)	Small	Medium	Large	Indoors/ Outdoors	Field
Business					
Industry					
Education					
Entertainment/ communication					
Health					
Government					
Military					

5. Personal skills checklist

Evaluate yourself, your human relations skills, and your ability to handle data and things, by checking the appropriate column.

	Good	Could improve
A. Evaluate yourself.		
Appearance/dress appropriate to the workplace	____	____
Manage needs and wants without interfering with the rights of others	____	____
Control impulses and feelings; channel energy in an effective way	____	____
Confidence level	____	____
B. How well do you interact with others?		
Respond with tact and courtesy	____	____
Accept criticism without anger	____	____
Respect, respond to, encourage, and compliment the ideas and good work of others	____	____
Share with and assist others	____	____
Honest, admit mistakes, willing to apologize	____	____
C. How well do you deal with data/things?		
Able to manage own time and work without asking many questions or needing much outside help	____	____
Able to try new and unfamiliar things; flexible	____	____
Punctual and responsible in carrying through on work —not making excuses even if work is difficult or unpleasant	____	____
Take good care of property	____	____
Follow rules, help make them more effective, reasonable	____	____

6. The bottom line

I plan to be employed in the job of my choice by (date) _____

The job *must* have at least the following:

1. Duties: _____

_____

2. Salary: _____

3. Work schedule: _____

4. Work environment: _____

_____

5. Benefits: _____

_____

6. What else? _____

_____

I will *not* accept a job that: _____

Eight Work affects the soul:

A philosophic view

Without work all life goes rotten. But when work is soulless, life stifles and dies. —Albert Camus

Work can be rewarding, exciting, fulfilling, exasperating, exhausting, and dreadful—sometimes all at once. Work is often hard work!

Work affects the nation and the world, as well as the individual. To see where we all fit into the picture—and whether we like what we see—we will now reflect on the larger view and the longer run.

A global view of work

What is work? There are many definitions, including some that overlap or contradict. Without getting too technical and precise, let's say that work is activity that provides goods and services to others while providing some reward for the worker.

Unless forced, we humans don't do anything without motivation. And our motivators are our needs and wants. Most people work for money to fulfill their various needs in the hierarchy as seen by Maslow. Those with enough resources to fulfill their basic needs then work for other reasons. A housewife works to care for husband and children. Her rewards may vary from love and mutual support to avoidance of disapproval.

Some people work because the work is intrinsically satisfying to their personalities. Others go to work to be with people, get noticed, be approved, and for a whole host of unique and individual enticements. But along the way, work must also be useful to others.

Day and night the world hums with the activities of people and machines making goods for one another. Mines and forests, oceans and fields yield raw substances to make a myriad of *things*. Wood and metal, coal and cotton, and thousands of other materials are baled and baked, pounded and pummeled, mixed

159

and milled, cut and checked, piled and packed for delivery to the world. Trucks and trains, planes and ships move endlessly huffing and hauling it all to other factories and farms, stores and homes.

Things! They are bought, sold, used, recycled, worn out, and finally discarded to become endless piles of debris. Some of it returns to the earth, some of it remains to pollute and plague us.

Along with the production of goods, work involves those often intangible "services rendered." From answering phones and directing traffic to designing systems and supervising workers, more and more people are involved in trans-actions: interactions, communications, "deals."

We seem to be struggling into a new era that emphasizes *data* and *people* over *things*. The things are made more easily than ever before because technology saves us from many back-breaking tasks. But our view of this change is limited because we are accustomed to having *more* things—more than any other country on earth. We take them for granted. Many affluent people cluster in suburbs believing they are average Americans, while "average Americans" look mighty prosperous to much of the world. Transactional society, in which transaction jobs predominate over production jobs, accounts for only a small percentage of the world.

Basically, the human race needs food, clothing, and shelter to survive. Some human beings do not survive because they lack even these most basic necessities. As population expands, societies that were once self-sustaining are no longer able to supply their own necessities. Trade and travel arose very early in human history in response to the need for imported goods. But even today, transportation of basic goods is a necessity sadly lacking in many parts of the world. For example, it is said that much of India's hunger problem would be solved if the large quantities of food produced in one part of the country had adequate transport to needy areas.

While great numbers of the world's people barely subsist, the affluent countries produce luxuries unheard of even by the most powerful emperors of old. Many very ordinary children own television sets, stereos, calculators, ten-speed bikes, and other magical, wonderful gadgets.

As a nation we have entered an era of affluence and high living standards never before seen in all of history. In two centuries we have changed from an agrarian society, involved with simple necessities, to a technically oriented one involved with complex necessities and many luxuries. We are the richest nation on earth; we use the most energy and resources per capita of any country. And our powerful influence causes others to rush to imitate us.

But the provision of goods and services (called *work*), to those willing to pay for them, is costly in more than dollars and souls. It is costing us dearly in terms of irreplaceable energy and resources and in irreversible damage to the environment. The United States seems to be leading the world on a collision course with nature.

Decisions are needed, but we don't see clearly what to decide. Every possible choice causes some group somewhere to protest. Environmentalists vie with labor, and labor struggles with government, as government conflicts with business over their special interests. And the resulting tension and fear of the future affect us all as we try to see our own personal direction. Work affects our souls!

We are at an exciting crossroads where careful choices could create a better world. But there are no simple answers. So far, individuals' suggested alternatives have resounded like voices crying in the wilderness. Buckminster Fuller shows us complex geometric dwellings; Paolo Soleri builds a strange city in the desert; E. F. Schumacher says "intermediate technology" might be more humane and waste less energy.

Little by little, however, the message is becoming clear: decisions are in order. But before decisions can be made, values must be clarified. First we must know what we need and want and we must realize what our wants will cost in larger terms. To line up our values, we might agree that work should be self-fulfilling, leisurely, meaningful activity that produces worthwhile products and services through peaceful, nonpolluting, resource-conserving methods. We are surprised that not everyone agrees what these products and services shall be. Such issues have social, political, and economic ramifications. For example, *peaceful* means "peace-keeping" to many people. And thus the national defense budget consumes just about 60 percent of the personal income tax collected yearly. We may agree to provide services to our weaker members: the disabled, the elderly, the needy minorities, the unwanted young, the uneducated, the poor, the imprisoned. But then our tax bill comes and we rebel.

Perhaps corporations could cut down on profits. But this "remedy" strikes at the heart of the free enterprise system, and many companies are on a slim profit margin as it is.

Any move we make to cut back will change or short-change the money flow in some way. In the extreme view, we are caught in a bind of building/producing/ doing more and more of what we could perhaps use less and less of. We exhaust ourselves and the environment to keep the economy going.

When we get to the ultimate point (the one just before "no return"), will we have to start paying to dismantle it all? Garrett DeBell fantasizes this happening in "A Future that Makes Ecological Sense."[1] Maybe it has already started. A parking lot in Yosemite National Park has been turned into a meadow!

At any rate, a national and global clarification of values continues. Your individual soul-searching will add to the pool of collective consciousness. Again, how much of what things do you want and need? How do your choices fit the global view? How do these choices affect your soul?

A personal view of work

As we look at the work world we've created, a little question keeps arising: What is all this frantic activity achieving for *you*? What is happening to the individual in the midst of it all?

First, subtle changes have separated us from natural things. We drive and park along heavily concreted wastelands. Many people work in buildings without windows, far from sunlight and breezes.

We work on schedules that don't accord with our natural rhythms. We are continually caught in a time bind in an increasingly complex world of ever longer commutes, more complicated personal business transactions, more involved maintenance of homes and gadgets. Most people work on a rigid schedule with little leeway for personal needs.

HERMAN *by Unger*

Listen, if you want to eat in the office, BRING SANDWICHES!

Many people are convinced that such stress even causes death. In the book *Type A Behavior and Your Heart*, Friedman and Rosenman deal with behavior characteristics of the heart-attack-prone individual. We see a profile of the striving American doing six things at once and all the while fearing failure.[2]

Our biology tries to catch up with our technology. We have much evolving to do to learn to blend with technology without losing our identities. Yet it would hardly be feasible to give it all up. We need technology. How about "biorhythmic technology"—moderated and more humane?

Second, work takes time. It can occupy a large part of a day, a week, a year, a lifetime. For many people the forty-hour week and the fifty-week year are the center of life. Flexibility for many is nonexistent and leisure, hard won. But John Kenneth Galbraith says, "Only if an individual has a choice as to the length of his working week or year, along with the option of taking unpaid leave for longer periods, does he or she have an effective choice between income and leisure."[3]

Many people feel that work uses too much prime time. Work plus family demands and the "business of living" leave one with little time for other enriched choices. Studs Terkel quotes a steelworker who says, "If I had a twenty-hour work-week, I'd get to know my kids better, my wife better. Some kid invited me to go on a college campus. On a Saturday. It was summertime. Hell, if I have a choice of taking my wife and kids to a picnic or going to a college campus, it's gonna be the picnic. But if I worked a twenty-hour week, I could do both. Don't you think with that extra twenty hours people could really expand?"[4]

Many workplaces creak with rigidity. For example, most employers are fearful of letting people leave work early when they are caught up. To avoid such struggles, the forty-hour week has become sacrosanct and is further regulated by professional and union rules about who does what when. Thus, it is reported that the workers in a little state office in one small midwestern town, when they occasionally finish all assigned work at 4 or 4:30, don hats and coats and sit in their darkened office until 5 o'clock. Probably they use the time to worry about children at home alone and what to have for supper.

A secretary at one of the world's largest corporations sits at her desk at 11:30 A.M. facing a day with little or no work because of a slowdown. Asked if she is permitted to go home early in such a case, she is horrified. "Never, in a company like this!" With a spectacular view of San Francisco, its bay, ocean, and bridges all around, she sits surrounded by little portable walls, seeing nothing, doing nothing. To knit or read a good book—even a book on how to be a better secretary— would violate a "no-no." What a strain to fear being seen without work lest one's job disappear!

In order to relieve worker boredom, management psychologists have tried to diversify tasks, but such measures have limited value when the tasks themselves remain repetitive and dull. Psychologists have also attempted to give workers more autonomy by including them in the decision-making process. Robert Schrank, a Ford Foundation work specialist, believes that such attempts are likely to be fruitless. Schrank, who has worked on an assembly line himself, points out that every detail is predetermined in a modern production line. The workers canno⁴ introduce variations.

Schrank suggests that workers, especially blue-collar people, be allowed time to socialize on the job, if they can still complete their work on time. He uses the word "schmooze" to describe the amenities that professional and white-collar workers enjoy: time to make a phone call, talk with co-workers, take some extra time off at lunch. "Schmooze time" would relieve some of the boredom inherent in many production jobs. Schrank believes these minor privileges would be more rewarding to the worker than diversified tasks or other current attempts at motivation.[5]

The late Hal Boyle of Associated Press estimated that most people who spend eight hours in their offices could get their required work done in two hours.[6] And

Tony Shively (pen name, Thorne Lee), writer and philosopher, says, "The average person is only capable of four productive hours of work a day. The rest is spent filling time. Society often demands more of a man's nature than he can give." In a walk through many workplaces, one can observe people finished with their four essential hours. One of James Michener's characters advises a young man in *The Fires of Spring*, "A lot of nonsense is spoken about work. Some of the finest men I've known were the laziest. Never work because it's expected of you. Find out how much work you must do to live and be happy. Don't do any more."[7]

Flexible time experiments

Some experimentation with new work schedules is being done. Flextime, for example, allows workers to work for any eight hours between specified times, such as 7 A.M. to 6 P.M. Absenteeism drops and productivity rises. People can take care of "the business of life" in their off-hours when others are still at work to serve them. Those whose biorhythms make them either early or late risers are accommodated. Four ten-hour days per week is a variation on flextime that has yielded similar good results. Some companies are even experimenting with three twelve-hour shifts, enabling college students to work three week-end nights and still attend classes.

Job sharing enables people to choose shorter work hours while getting the job done with a partner. Again, research shows that absenteeism drops and productivity rises. Some companies allow people to work at home on their own time. All such flexibility, it must be noted, adds to the work and cost of management.

Not everyone could slow down and enjoy leisure even if it were more available. For some, work is life. Instead of getting in touch with other facets of their personalities, the total technologist eschews social gatherings; the confirmed clerk avoids art. In the extreme, a highly successful person could be leading a life impoverished on many levels.

And yet many more people could be employed if some people worked fewer than forty hours per week, fifty weeks per year. The loss of income might be offset in many ways (even financially): saving energy and resources, enjoying a more enriched life, having more time for the business of living.[8]

Most people, especially males, begin work after graduating from high school or college and keep at it until age 65. Even the most exciting of career fields can pall after many years. Steps must often be taken to keep up one's motivation. Going back to school, looking for promotions, changing positions or companies, looking for a unique approach to one's job, finding enriching hobbies, all help to keep up one's energy. Some industries have experimented with leaves of absence for social action projects and part-time or full-time educational leaves, either paid or unpaid.

For some people the opportunity to work after age 65 is most welcome. To others retirement (as early as possible) means liberation to do other things. We are just barely beginning to consider the possibility of integrating work and leisure. Some husbands are taking time off while wives work; some people are "easing into retirement" with reduced schedules. Total involvement in work then may not be essential in an affluent, transactional society.

Most workers have experienced the two extremes—either total work or no work —instead of a balance of the two. But in 1969 we passed the era of full employment based on a forty-hour week. Now we need creative schemes that will enable business, industry, and government to train larger numbers of workers for fewer hours of work per week. The cost will be great, but the benefits might be even greater. In a work-oriented society, where the unemployed feel inadequate, crime and mental illness increase when the unemployment rate is high. The quality of life is diminished. Taxes must be increased to pay for welfare and related problems, including law enforcement and health care.

Autonomy dimensions

Closely related to some people's need for flexible time is the need for autonomy. People appreciate having some say in what happens to their souls and bodies during the work day. Alienation is less prevalent when people feel involved in decision-making. Some autonomy can do a lot to ease systems pained at all levels, global to personal.

The kinds of decisions we are referring to are the really *major* ones, of course, like who will go to lunch when, who can have the best typewriter, and how many times a day you can use the copier. These are the decisions that affect personnel personally, where it hurts, in the every day.

The *minor* decisions include whether to expand company operations into Pakistan, invest a million in a new widget/gidget, or buy a shipping line. The majority of workers will be touched by these types of decisions only in that less sensitive spot called "the long run," which is not today. What directly affects *me now* has a high-level priority.

Management training today is geared to decision-making teams. More worker involvement is seen as a plus in increasing productivity. It's especially valuable when supported by profit and benefit sharing. Communications skills are the key to effectiveness in today's management. The openness required to encourage trust feels like a risk and requires constant encouragement and much sensitivity to human needs. But the majority of people (even small children) respond responsibly when given a chance.

The alternative, an arbitrary use of power, can stifle growth and initiative and defeat the ultimate goals of the workplace. But workplaces tend to be conservative. "Work is hard work" and is a serious enterprise mainly geared to profit and/or public service. Shared decision-making means we have to *think, adapt, relate, create,* which takes *time* . . . and *time* is *money.* What is more, some workers would like to keep the status quo and not get too involved. Joe Rodriquez, age 36, a ten-year Ford employee took part in an experiment at Saab Engine Plant in Sweden designed to maximize worker involvement in decision making. Said Joe, "If I've got to bust my ass to be meaningful, forget it. I'd rather be monotonous."[9] Thus, tension arises between employers' needs to get on with it and their dependence on worker goodwill to get the job done. It will probably always be so. There is need for the right balance. But the human potential is there waiting to be tapped by creative, positive leadership in cooperation with workers. It's a lofty goal, perhaps, but one worth aiming for.

The work ethic

Today many people are beginning to question the work ethic that is part of our American heritage. Work is necessary, of course, and sometimes enjoyable. "However, there is no intrinsic virtue in work in and of itself," according to Terrance E. Carroll. He believes that "virtue is attached to it by individual attitudes that have been learned, and the fact that a great many individuals in our society share that attitude does not mean either that all people should share it, or that it is even a healthy attitude for all who do. The human personality is capable of enjoyment and was meant to enjoy, not merely to consume; to create, not merely to produce."[10]

Not everyone shares Carroll's attitude toward work, of course. (Thar's them 'ats fer it, 'n them 'ats agin it.) A strong work ethic stems from early colonial days, when "Idleness is the Devil's workshop" was a truth not to be questioned, like Ben Franklin's dictum that "Time is money." Americans value those who have "made it," and look down upon poor achievers with feelings ranging from compassion to moral outrage. People should do their work as a God-given duty, and only then can they expect a just reward: happiness and a home in the suburbs. So goes the common principle. Thus by and large we are work addicts—striving, struggling, even being ruthless and immoral to succeed. (*Work* sometimes becomes the Devil's workshop!)

The backlash from our national policies and attitudes was described in *Work in America*, a 1972 Special Task Force report to the Secretary of Health, Education, and Welfare:

> Because work is central to the lives of most Americans, either the absence of work or employment in meaningless work is creating an increasingly intolerable situation. The human costs of this state of affairs are manifested in worker alienation, alcoholism, drug addiction, and other symptoms of poor mental health. Moreover, much of our tax money is expended in an effort to compensate for problems with at least a part of their genesis in the world of work. A great part of the staggering national bill in the areas of crime and delinquency, mental, physical health, manpower and welfare are generated in our national policies and attitudes towards work. Likewise, industry is paying for its continued attachment to Tayloristic practices through low worker productivity and high rates of sabotage, absenteeism, and turnover. Unions are paying through the faltering loyalty of a young membership that is increas-

ingly concerned about the apparent disinterest of its leadership in problems of job satisfaction. Most important, there are the high costs of lost opportunities to encourage citizen participation: the discontent of women, minorities, blue-collar workers, youth, and older adults would be considerably less were these Americans to have had an active voice in the decisions in the workplace that most directly affect their lives.[11]

Mainly, however, we seem to be in a period of rising expectations about ourselves and work. Well, why not? Why not expand our vision? "The true person is as yet a dream of the future." Why keep that idea forever in the future? Why not make it present reality? The premise of this manual is that work, and maybe even life, can be joy!

If we can find a place where we feel some measure of success, some value, we shall find new energy to put into our work. Dr. Hans Selye talks about the relationship between aging, work, and stress: "Work wears you out mainly through the frustrations of failure. Most of the eminent among hard workers in almost any field lived a long life. Since work is a basic need of man, the question is not whether to work but what kind of work is play."[12] And Yehudi Menuhin expresses it best when he says, "All my life I have reveled in the sound of the violin."

We have many resources of mind and spirit. Can we move to a place of more joy in work and in life? Personal growth is essential. Each person can help by expanding his/her awareness of self and others. We seem to long for a less pressured, more serene life, with less frantic activity. Busy people are asserting their need for daily meditation, yoga, or other forms of relaxation to help them get in touch with deeper values.

In this chapter we have merely touched the surface of a few of the concerns, global and personal, that relate to work. But each individual must garner the courage to fashion a meaningful existence, to find the balance between personal needs and the needs of others. We are responsible to ourselves for the quality of our own lives. We can be friends or enemies to ourselves by the choices we make, which in turn make up the lives we live. Real caring about ourselves is the first step in caring for others and in solving global concerns.

May your career choice contribute to your dream of the future.

 **EXERCISES:** WORK

A. Group discussion

   1. What were the last three things you've purchased? What basic needs did they fulfill? What wants? Could you get along without them for a year?

2. What things that are produced do you consider useless?

3. How does producing an apple commercially cause pollution? Think of ten ways. Which of these factors would still be present if you grew the apple organically in your yard?

4. How is making a phone call involved with energy resources and pollution? Think of ten ways. Rate on a scale of 1 to 10 how necessary you think the telephone is in our society? Why?

5. List all the devices you have at home that use electricity. On a scale of 1 to 10, rate how necessary each appliance is to you. If you could use only five, which ones would you choose?

6. Fantasize what it would be like if you had to keep *all* your discards and throw nothing away. What changes would you make in your life?

7. In what ways does technology (and the resulting modern life) conflict with your biology?

8. What do you feel is the best way to relieve worker boredom and monotony?

9. What is "schmooze" time? How would you like to use it on the job if you could?

10. How much responsibility would you like for planning your own work routine?

11. Describe your ideal boss.

12. Do you prefer working alone, or with a team? Why?

13. What is the relationship between a good career choice and world harmony?

14. What will motivate you to work?

15. Can we all "get to the top"? What are the limits of that reality, and how can you deal with it?

B. Discuss the following, either in a notebook or in a written report.

1. What meaning does work have for you?

2. Design an ideal job.

3. Describe your ideal work day, week, year, lifetime.

4. Describe your ideal balance of work and leisure.

5. What is your personal work ethic?

6. How does your career choice fit your value system?

7. How does your value system fit in with world needs?

8. What social problem would you most like to see solved in your lifetime? How could your career choice help to solve it?

9. What has this chapter helped you to learn about yourself?

10. What is the most significant thing this book has helped you to learn about yourself?

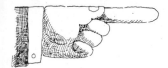 # The final analysis

Look again at your answers to the exercises at the end of each chapter. What did you learn about yourself by completing these exercises? Summarize your discoveries in the spaces provided below.

Chapter 1

Tapping into feelings—Review your feelings about yourself, various groups of people, and your life circumstances. List six things you would like to change.

1.
2.
3.
4.
5.
6.

Needs and wants—Review your survival needs, people needs, and fulfillment needs. List six important areas for change.

1.
2.
3.
4.
5.
6.

Exploring your values—Review your enjoyment values. List the five activities that you enjoy the most.

1.
2.
3.
4.
5.

Review your life values, personal trait values, and career values. List your three most important values in each category.

Life values	*Personal trait values*	*Career values*
1.	1.	1.
2.	2.	2.
3.	3.	3.

Your accomplishments—List your six most satisfying accomplishments.

1.
2.
3.
4.
5.
6.

Chapter 2

Your roles—List three roles you hope to assume and jot down a brief description of each.

1.
2.
3.

Chapter 3

A career or "Just a job"? Which do you choose and why?

Chapter 4

Personality mosaic—List your Personality Types in the order of the three highest scores.

1. _____
2. _____
3. _____

Data, people, things involvement indicator—Rate Hi, Med, or Lo and explain why.

Data

People

Things

Work qualities inventory—Write out your "must have" work qualities.

1.
2.
3.
4.
5.

Skills analysis—Are you a "mind person," "body person," or both? _____
List your five most important skills.

1.

2.

3.

4.

5.

Job groups—List job groups from the Job Group Chart in the order of your own
interests.

1.

2.

3.

Use the *Guide for Occupational Exploration* to answer the next six questions about your
top job group.

1. Explain why you chose your top job group. How does it match your personality, skills,
   and interests?

2. Summarize the kind of work you would do.

3. Summarize skills and abilities you would need for this kind of work.

4. Summarize clues that tell you whether you would like or could learn this work.

5. Summarize the training you would need and the usual methods of entry into this field.

6. Will any of the college majors that you checked in Chapter 4·provide the training you need? If so, which ones?

7. Look up one job title from your job group in the *Dictionary of Occupational Titles.* Write a short summary of this job.

Chapter 5

Employment outlook—What is the employment outlook for the career of your choice?

What is the salary range? _____   Will it support your lifestyle? _____

Describe your ideal workplace, using your feelings and findings from your research.

1. Size and complexity
2. Important physical features
3. Important psychological features (i.e., how "human" it is)

Chapter 7

Personal skills checklist—List your good skills and the skills you could improve.

	Good skills	Could improve
1		
2		
3.		
4.		
5.		
6.		

What is your "next move?"

Educational planning sheet

1. Do you now have the skills you need to obtain a job in the field of your choice?

   _____ yes   _____ no

   If you need more preparation, which of the following do you need?

   _____ apprenticeship
   _____ on-the-job training
   _____ workshops or seminars
   _____ other: _____

2. If you need more education, which of the following are you considering?

   _____ a few courses
   _____ a certificate
   _____ AA/AS
   _____ BA/BS
   _____ graduate school
   _____ other: _____

3. List an appropriate major (or majors) for your career choice.

4. What kind of school do you plan to attend?

   _____ two-year
   _____ four-year
   _____ local college
   _____ college in your state
   _____ out-of-state college
   _____ public
   _____ private

5. Below, list colleges or universities that offer the major you have chosen. (Use the educational reference section of your library, and ask for assistance from a college counseling center.)

6. Obtain catalogs for colleges of interest. To gather as much information as possible, visit the campuses, talk to people who are familiar with each school. For example, will you need

_____ financial aid

_____ housing

_____ special entrance tests

_____ a specific GPA

_____ other: _____

7. Begin course planning in the space below.

Major requirements	General or graduation requirements	Electives
_____	_____	_____
_____	_____	_____
_____	_____	_____
_____	_____	_____

Review all of the inventories you have taken. Read your autobiography again.
Check each item in "The Final Analysis" to make sure there are no contradictions.

Does it hang together?   Yes _____   No _____

What are you going to do with your life? _____

Why?

✳ ✳ ✳ ✳ ✳ ✳ ✳ ✳ ✳ ✳ ✳ ✳

HANG LOOSE
Michele F. Bakarich

I'm

just

going

to

hang

loose

,

that's

the

best

way

to

go

Notes

Chapter 1

1. Abraham Maslow, *Motivation and Personality* (New York: Harper and Row, 1954), p. 91; *see also* Marilyn M. Bates and Clarence Johnson, *A Manual for Group Leaders* (Denver: Love Publishing, 1972); and Ken Keyes, Jr., *Handbook to Higher Consciousness* (St. Mary's, Ky.: Cornucopia Institute, 1975).
2. Nena O'Neill and George O'Neill, *Shifting Gears* (New York: Avon, 1974), p. 140.
3. Keyes, *op. cit.*, p. 52.
4. Cf. Gary Carnum, "Everybody Talks about Values," *Learning*, December 1972; and S. B. Simon, S. W. Howe, and H. Kirschenbaum, *Values Clarification* (New York: Hart, 1972).
5. Simon et al., *op. cit.*, pp. 30, 113-115.

Chapter 2

1. Virginia Y. Trotter, "Women in Leadership and Decision Making: A Shift in Balance," *Vital Speeches*, 1 April 1975, pp. 373-375.
2. Pat Ackley, "Women and Work Questionnaire" (Fremont, Calif.: John F. Kennedy High School, 1976).
3. Ruth B. Kundsin, ed., *Women and Success: The Anatomy of Achievement* (New York: William Morrow, 1974), p. 176.
4. Bess Myerson, "Someday I'd Like to Walk Slowly," *Redbook*, September 1975, p. 76.
5. Alice Cook, "The Working Mother," address to Center for Research on Women, Stanford University, January 1976.
6. Aletha Huston Stein and Margaret M. Bailey, "The Socialization of Achievement Orientation in Females," *Psychological Bulletin* 80, no. 5 (November 1973): 353.
7. Caryl Rivers, *San Francisco Chronicle*, January 1, 1975.
8. Studs Terkel, *Working* (New York: Avon, 1972).
9. Lillian Hellman, *An Unfinished Woman: A Memoir* (Boston: Little, Brown, 1969).
10. Tish Sommers, "When Sexism Meets Ageism," *Modern Maturity*, October-November 1975, p. 60.
11. U.S. Dept. of Commerce, Bureau of the Census, *Statistical Abstracts of the United States*, 1978, p. 452.

12. Marilyn Power Goldberg, "The Economic Exploitation of Women," *Review of Radical Political Economics* 2, no. 1 (Spring 1970).
13. J. K. Galbraith, "The Economics of the American Housewife," *Harpers*, June 1973, p. 78.

Chapter 3

1. John L. Holland, *Making Vocational Choices: A Theory of Careers* (Englewood Cliffs, N.J.: Prentice-Hall, 1973).
2. Edward Gross, "Patterns of Organizational and Occupational Socialization," *The Vocational Guidance Quarterly*, December 1975, p. 140.
3. Ray A. Killian, "The Working Woman . . . A Male Manager's View," American Management Ass'n, 1971.
4. Estell Buchanan, "For Women, A Difficult Climb to the Top," *Business Week*, 2 August 1969, pp. 42–44.
5. Irving Goffman, *Asylums* (New York: Doubleday, 1961).
6. Barbara Garson, "Women's Work," *Working Papers*, Fall 1973, p. 5.

Chapter 4

1. John L. Holland, *Making Vocational Choices: A Theory of Careers* (Englewood Cliffs, N.J.: Prentice-Hall, 1973).
2. U.S. Department of Labor, *Dictionary of Occupational Titles*, 1978.
3. U.S. Department of Labor, *Guide for Occupational Exploration*, 1979.
4. U.S. Department of Labor, *Dictionary of Occupational Titles*, vol. 2, 1965; U.S. Department of Labor, *Guide for Occupational Exploration*, 1979; U.S. Army, *Career and Education Guide*, Counselor Edition, 1978; U.S. Department of Labor, *Handbook for Analyzing Jobs*, 1972.

Chapter 5

1. Jean Gottman, *Megalopolis* (Cambridge, Mass.: M.I.T. Press, 1973).
2. U.S. Department of Labor, *Occupational Outlook Handbook*, 1978.
3. U.S. Department of Labor, *Manpower Report of the President*, 1974.
4. Leonard Lecht, *Education and Work*, 27 January 1976, p. 5.
5. U.S. Department of Labor, "Job Outlook in Brief," *Career Guidance Magazine*, 1978.
6. Walter Chandoha, *Book of Kittens and Cats* (New York: Bramhall House, 1973), p. 8.
7. Phyllis Harris, "How to Earn Extra $," *Family Circle*, May 1975, p. 2.

Chapter 6

1. Jeremy Main, "Ten Terrific Companies to Work For," *Money*, November 1976, p. 44.
2. Toni St. James, Interview Workshop, California Employment Development Department, 1977.

Chapter 8

1. Garrett DeBell, "A Future that Makes Ecological Sense," *The Environmental Handbook* (New York: Ballantine Books, 1970), p. 153–158.

2. Meyer Friedman and Ray H. Rosenman, *Type A Behavior and Your Heart* (New York: Fawcett, 1974).
3. John Kenneth Galbraith, "The Economics of an American Housewife," *Atlantic Monthly*, August 1973, pp. 78–83.
4. Terkel, *Working*, p. 4.
5. Robert Schrank, "How to Relieve Worker Boredom," *Psychology Today*, July 1978, pp. 79–80.
6. Charles McCabe, *San Francisco Chronicle*, September 1974.
7. James Michener, *The Fires of Spring* (New York: Bantam Books, 1949).
8. Fred Best, "Recycling People: Work Sharing Through Flexible Life Scheduling," *Futurist*, February 1978, p. 8.
9. *Time*, 10 March 1975, p. 42.
10. Terrance E. Carroll, "The Ideology of Work," *Vocational Guidance Quarterly*, December 1975, p. 140.
11. U.S. Department of Health, Education, and Welfare, *Work in America* (Cambridge, Mass.: M.I.T. Press, 1973), pp. 186–187.
12. Hans Selye, *Stress Without Distress* (Philadelphia: J. B. Lippincott, 1974).

Index

183